POCKET KIWI

So you think you know
New Zealand?

Rosemary Hepözden

NEW
HOLLAND

Dedication

To Jacob Hepözden - always number one on my list.

First published in 2019 by New Holland Publishers
Auckland • Sydney

newhollandpublishers.com

Level 1, 178 Fox Valley Road, Wahroonga 2076, Australia
5/39 Woodside Ave, Northcote, Auckland 0627, New Zealand

Rosemary Hepözden has asserted her right to be identified as the author of this work.

Publisher: Sarah Beresford
Editor: Elise James
Design: Yolanda La Gorcé
Production Director: Arlene Gippert

A catalogue record for this book is available from the National Library of New Zealand

ISBN 9781869665425

1 3 5 7 9 10 8 6 4 2

Printed in China by Toppan Leefung Printing Ltd, on paper sourced from sustainable forests.

Keep up with New Holland Publishers:

 NewHollandPublishers
 @newhollandpublishers

Contents

Introduction

It starts in primary school with a spelling list and continues right up to the bucket list of old age. In between, there are to-do lists, shopping lists, packing lists, guest lists, gift lists, inventory lists, checklists, wedding lists, wish lists …

Lists are how we record, organize, understand and recall everything we need to remember.

There's even lists for stuff we didn't know we needed to remember – until we get stuck for conversation around the dinner table, want to impress someone with obscure details and offbeat opinions, sign up for pub quiz nights, or just want a refreshing way of viewing familiar facts. This is where *Pocket Kiwi: So you think you know New Zealand?* comes in.

To refresh our memory of what New Zealand is all about, we should list everything that's right under our noses. No subject is too big or too small, too obvious or too offbeat. The lists here explore the entire range of Kiwi life, from why so few people have a birthday on Waitangi Day and why Kiri Te Kanawa has reason to feel sad, right through to which cafés to sit in if you want to meet a Kiwi songwriter and what books prisoners are borrowing from the library.

By presenting thousands of facts in memorable form, I hope you find that New Zealand becomes a richer, funnier and more inspiring place to live. *Kiwi as!*

Rosemary Hepōzden

About the Author

Rosemary Hepözden has spent years reading and writing about New Zealand but has only recently stumbled on the realisation that the older we get, the more we need to remember, therefore the more lists we need to keep. This book presents Kiwi life in list form – an abbreviated version of events in the intriguing little land in which we live.

Other books written by Rosemary Hepözden include *The Daily Male: A Kiwi Bloke's Book of Days; Instant Kiwi: New Zealand in a Nutshell;* and *Sorted: A Curious Kiwi Book of Lists*, all published by New Holland Publishers (NZ).

Chapter

One

New Zealand

PEOPLE and PLACES:

Heroes and Heartland

DAYS THAT CHANGED NEW ZEALAND

29 May 1953: Ed Hillary reaches the top of Mt Everest

Ed Hillary and Tenzing Norgay become the first men to summit Mt Everest, the world's highest peak. Sir Ed devotes the rest of his life to helping the Sherpa people of Nepal, using his international celebrity to raise funds to build many schools and hospitals. He does much more than give Kiwis something to be proud of. His example of humility – on his descent from the summit he announced simply, 'Well, George, we knocked the bastard off' – becomes ingrained in the national psyche as a mindset worth cultivating no matter how magnificent the achievement. Humility becomes the permanent hallmark of decent Kiwi character.

6 FAMOUS TREVORS

Our favourite comic creation, deadpan farmer Fred Dagg had 'approximately half a dozen' sons, all called Trevor. ('Very good boys they were, too. Especially Trevor.') It's never been confirmed, but possibly they were all born in 1954, when Trevor ranked at number 34 – between Colin and Kenneth – on the list of popular names for boys. Besides the Trevor Daggs, here are a few memorable real-life Trevors (approximately half a dozen).

◊ The richest is former supermarket checkout operator Trevor Cooper, whose lucky Lotto ticket won him $27 million in 2012. 'Nothing is going to change,' he proclaimed. He turned up to his wedding hunched over a Harley Davidson with a fag hanging out of his mouth, and later splashed out very publicly on off-road racing cars and bikes and a dozen properties. Despite his wealth, not all was happy in his world. Within three years, his marriage had folded. There was no pre-nup, because his mother had advised him one wasn't necessary 'if you love them and they love you'.

◊ Trevor Richards founded the anti-apartheid movement HART (Halt All Racist Tours) in 1969 and eventually got to ask Nelson Mandela for his autograph at a fireworks display in the Auckland Domain in 1995.

◊ Trevor Manning was goalkeeper for New Zealand's field hockey team at the Montreal Olympics in 1976. Fourteen minutes before the end of the final against Australia, his kneecap was smashed by a flying puck. After doing a couple of squats 'to show the Aussies there was nothing wrong', Manning continued playing and the kiwis went on to win the gold medal.

◊ Trevor Lloyd was a graphic artist who, in 1905, drew one of the first New Zealand cartoons using the kiwi as a symbol for New Zealand. He is also credited with coming up with the term 'snail mail' to describe postal delivery.

◊ Trevor Nash was sentenced to 10 years' imprisonment for his part in a £20,000 payroll robbery in Auckland in 1956. He escaped from jail, fled the country and remained free for six months. When he was eventually arrested in Melbourne, he said, 'God, you wouldn't read about it.'

◊ The most visually spectacular was Trevor Rupe, a farmer's son from Taumarunui who became the flamboyant drag queen Carmen, hostess of Carmen's International Coffee Lounge in Wellington in 1967.

After announcing publicly that certain MPs were hiding their homosexual orientation, she was required to appear before the Parliamentary Privileges Committee to discuss the allegations. Carmen turned up to parliament in a black chauffeur-driven limousine. 'Bulbs were flashing all around,' she said, 'and I was pleased that I had taken my white fox fur stole along with me.'

... and one Trevor the Aussies can keep

◊ Trevor Chappell. On 1 February 1981, when Australia was playing New Zealand in a One Day International at the Melbourne Cricket Ground, Chappell delivered the final ball by rolling it along the ground to batsman Brian McKechnie, denying the New Zealanders the chance to try for the six runs that would tie the match. By doing so, Chappell single-handedly soured trans-Tasman relations for a very long time indeed.

3 NEW ZEALANDERS BORN ON WAITANGI DAY

Waitangi Day, 6 February, is a very uncommon birthday in New Zealand, ranking at number 360 out of a possible 366. The most common birthday is 30 September.

The low incidence of births on Waitangi Day and the high incidence of births at the end of September suggest a couple of social phenomena: during the first week of May (nine months before Waitangi Day), rivetingly good television takes priority over procreation - while New Year's Eve parties could account for a lot of reckless fun ... and September births.

When we celebrate Waitangi Day, we should also sing 'Happy Birthday' to three notable Kiwis:

◊ Eric Honeywood Partridge (born 1894, near Gisborne; died

1 June 1979, Devon, England). He wrote a lot about language – over 40 books, in fact, including the much-admired *Dictionary of Slang and Unconventional English*, published in 1937. *The New York Times Book Review* recognized its genius: 'The unmentionables are mentioned and carefully placed in proper alphabetical form', it noted.

◊ Barry Magee (born 1934, in New Plymouth, and still going strong). He was, by his own admission, 'a nothing and a nobody' until he joined a local harrier club. At age 17, he met Arthur Lydiard and started training alongside athletes like Peter Snell, Murray Halberg and Bill Baillie. In 1960 he won the bronze medal in the marathon at the Rome Olympics and, later that year, became the first Kiwi to win an overseas marathon, at Fukuoka in Japan, with a time of 2:19:04.

◊ Colin Albert Murdoch (born 1929, in Christchurch; died 4 May 2008, in Timaru). He was a particularly inventive pharmacist and veterinarian. As well as developing guns and darts for tranquillizing animals, he came up with the disposable hypodermic syringe as a way of preventing disease being transmitted from animal to animal or person to person. When he presented his syringe to the NZ Health Department, the idea was snootily dismissed as 'too futuristic'. Now, every year, over 16 billion plastic syringes are used worldwide.

... and 5 internationals born on Waitangi Day

◊ Ronald Reagan, former American president, born 1911

◊ Eva Braun, wife of Adolf Hitler, born 1912

- ◊ Zsa Zsa Gabor, nine-times-married Hungarian-born actress and socialite, born 1917

- ◊ Bob Marley, Jamaican reggae superstar, born 1945

- ◊ Axl Rose, lead vocalist of Guns N' Roses, born 1962

12 SKILLS OF THE PERFECT KIWI WOMAN

Ever since a Speight's beer advertisement reminded us that 'She's a hard road finding the perfect woman, boy', the hunt has continued. All joking aside, the annual Perfect Woman Competition in Wanaka raises significant funds for the CanLive Cancer Trust, which supports people in Central Otago who are living with cancer. Winning has nothing to do with good looks and everything to do with competence. The list of desirable talents varies each time, but often tests proficiency in:

- ◊ Opening a big bottle of beer with a chainsaw

- ◊ Crutching a sheep

- ◊ Backing a trailer

- ◊ Racing a jet ski

- ◊ Baking a batch of scones

- ◊ Straining a fence wire

- ◊ Cooking a steak

- ◊ Throwing a dart

- ◊ Skinning a possum

- ◊ Driving a digger

- ◊ Tying a tie on a man

◊ Picking up a slightly intoxicated
husband from the pub.

---

7 KIWIS IN THE PUBLIC EYE
WHOSE NAMES ARE HARD TO SPELL

◊ Denise L'Estrange-Corbet, fashion designer

◊ Golriz Ghahraman, Green Party politician

◊ Gordon Tietjens, former rugby sevens coach

◊ Phillip Tataurangi, golfer

◊ Ruud Kleinpaste, naturalist

◊ Urzila Carlson, comedian

◊ Zoi Sadowski-Synnott, snowboarder

---

8 PRODUCTS OF PALMY

Does everyone in Palmerston North think the world should be a better
place? The city has spawned politicians aplenty – Metiria Turei, David
Seymour, Steve Maharey and Grant Robertson among them – but let's,
for the moment, push the politicians aside. Let's even push the All Blacks
Aaron Cruden and Sam Whitelock aside. This list belongs to those
(some past, some present) whose noteworthiness – whose prominence
– is less fragile and transient.

◊ John Clarke, the creator of our beloved Fred Dagg, whose
trademark sayings ('Kick it in the guts, Trev!' and 'That'll be
the phone') entered the vernacular and still make us smile.
He penned New Zealand's alternative national anthem, 'We
Don't Know How Lucky We Are'.

◊ At the age of 30, Lloyd Morrison created an investment
bank that would found Infratil, an infrastructure investment

company that now owns, either wholly or partially, Trustpower, Z Energy, Wellington Airport and NZ Bus, among others. In 2003, he launched a campaign to change the flag of New Zealand and, in 2007, ranked at number 12 on the *New Zealand Listener* Power List.

◊ Gary Brain, originally a timpanist with the NZ Symphony Orchestra, never appeared embarrassed to be sitting at the back of the orchestra, occasionally striking the triangle. After a flight to the United States, when a suitcase fell from an overhead locker and crushed his wrist beyond repair, he retrained as a conductor.

◊ Meg Campbell, poet and wife of Alistair Campbell, struggled throughout her life with mental illness. But she flourished as a poet in the 1980s and continued to write until her death in 2007.

◊ Serial business entrepreneur Linda Jenkinson has made enough money to pay for the entire town. She was the second Kiwi ever to float a company on the United States Nasdaq stock exchange (for US$230 million), and she currently serves on the board of Air New Zealand. In 2016, Jenkinson was named a World Class New Zealander.

◊ Jacob Oram is a former international cricketer. Maybe it was his Palmy sense of humour, but when he injured his left ring finger in an ODI before the 2007 Cricket World Cup, he announced he would be willing to have the troublesome digit amputated if it meant he could play … Turns out he was just joking.

◊ Brendon Hartley, a professional racing driver, is the latest Palmy protégé claiming plenty of attention. As a kid, he began his motor racing career in kart tracing. In 2017, at the age of 27, he made his debut for Scuderia Toro Rosso at the United States Grand Prix, becoming only the ninth New Zealander to race in Formula One.

◊ Perhaps our favourite Palmy person is Madge Allsop, Dame Edna Everidge's long-suffering – and silent – bridesmaid in 14 episodes of the *Dame Edna Experience* in the late 1980s. Dame Edna would often explain Madge's drab and dreary demeanour in a cruel little aside to the audience: 'She's from Palmerston North.'

CHAMPION! THE CURIOUS CAPACITIES OF 7 KIWIS WHO HOLD GUINNESS WORLD RECORDS

Kiwis are renowned for their ingenuity, cultivated as a consequence of living far away from essential supplies and services and the ordinary pleasures of conventional theatre and music. But we do a lot more than climb mountains, win Grammys, produce world-famous wines, and send rockets into space. We entertain ourselves in unusual ways – so much so, that the pages of the *Guinness Book of World Records* are replete with reverence for more than a handful of outstanding exploits undertaken by notable local achievers:

◊ Stefan Paladin holds the record for eating the most whole sausages in one minute. He ingested eight whole sausages (each measuring 10 cm in length and 2 cm in width) in 60 seconds. Year awarded: 2001.

◊ Elliot Nicholls holds the record for the fastest time to send a prescribed text message while blindfolded. He texted 'The razor-toothed piranhas of the genera Serrasalmus and Pygocentrus are the most ferocious freshwater fish in the world. In reality they seldom attack a human' in just over 45 seconds. Year awarded: 2007.

◊ Wendy Jarnet holds the record for the largest collection of zebra-related items. Her collection of 508 objects includes a plastic wind-up zebra that bobs its head, spins its tail and jumps up and down. Year awarded: 2014.

◊ Lee Weir holds the record for most tattoos of the same cartoon character tattooed on the body. On his left arm he has 41 tattoos of Homer Simpson, including Homer as a donut. Year awarded: 2014.

◊ Angela Fredericks holds the record for the fastest time to open 100 mussels. She took 1 minute, 55.28 seconds to complete the challenge, beating her own record set the previous year. Year awarded: 2016.

◊ Blair Williamson holds the record for the most Rubik's Cubes solved while running a marathon. He solved the puzzle 254 times while completing the Christchurch International Marathon. Year awarded: 2017.

◊ Alastair Galpin, who was born in South Africa but moved to New Zealand in 2002, deserves a special mention. Acknowledged as the second biggest Guinness World Records breaker of the decade 2000–2009, he is known for producing the loudest clap, halving 10 matches with an axe in 2.86 seconds, and licking 57 stamps in one minute. His most conspicuously applauded triumph? The most 'high fives' in one minute (76 of them), earned in Auckland on 14 November 2009.

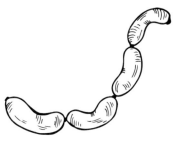

Smith & Co:
10 commonly uncommon Kiwis

The most common surname in New Zealand is Smith. That doesn't mean that the holders of the name share very much else. Consider, for example:

◊ Smith the Bilateral: Aaron Smith, famous as a brilliant All Blacks halfback, but infamous for pre-flight antics in a Christchurch Airport toilet.

◊ Smith the Cantankerous: Leighton Smith, political podcaster, who splutters audibly when anthropogenic climate change is mooted.

◊ Smith the Fanciful: Pink-haired Dot Smith, creator of Riverstone Castle, her medieval-themed dream home in north Otago.

◊ Smith the Linguist: Thomas H Smith, a judge in the Native Land Court who, in 1878, was the first to translate 'God Defend New Zealand' into te reo Maori.

◊ Smith the Mellifluous: Hollie Smith, chart-topping recording artist with a distinctive voice for jazz and soul.

◊ Smith the Sadly Missed: Kevin Smith, actor, best known as Ares, the dark and seductive Greek god of war, in the TV series *Hercules: The Legendary Journeys*.

◊ Smith the Slightly Subversive: Ron Smith was an active Communist who nevertheless maintained a solid career in straight-laced organizations. In 1970 he became senior research economist with the Department of Statistics. He died in 1995, before seeing his prediction come to pass that 'a new Marxist party with mass support will undoubtedly arise'.

- ◊ Smith the Socially Concerned: Fan Smith lived in Gore, where, in the 1930s, she kept herself very busy with good works. She was an active member of the Women's Christian Temperance Union and gave unflinching support to the children's charity Dr Barnardo's Homes.

- ◊ Smith the Storekeeper: Marianne Smith who, soon after arriving in Auckland from Ireland in 1880, opened Smith's Cheap Drapery Warehouse, which would eventually evolve into the enduring department store Smith & Caughey.

- ◊ Smith the Despicable: Phillip John Smith, convicted murderer and child sex offender, who received a payout of $3500 because his rights were found to have been breached when he was prevented from wearing his hairpiece in court.

THAT'S ABOUT THE SIZE OF IT:
16 REGIONAL COMPARISONS IN SQUARE KILOMETRES

Northland with Vanuatu	(12,498 and 12,190 respectively)
Auckland with Trinidad and Tobago	(4940 and 5130 respectively)
Waikato with Belize	(23,900 and 22,810 respectively)
Bay of Plenty with Fakland Islands	(12,071 and 12,173 respectively)
Gisborne with Puerto Rico	(8386 and 8870 respectively)
Hawke's Bay with Timor-Leste	(14,137 and 14,870 respectively)
Taranaki with the West Bank and Gaza	(7254 and 6020 respectively)
Manawatu with Israel	(22,221 and 21,640 respectively)
Wellington with Cyprus	(8049 and 9240 respectively)
Tasman with Jamaica	(9616 and 10,990 respectively)
Nelson with Barbados	(424 and 430 respectively)

Marlborough with Lebanon	(10,458 and 10,230 respectively)
West Coast with Djibouti	(23,244 and 23,180 respectively)
Canterbury with Estonia	(44,508 and 42,390 respectively)
Otago with Lesotho	(31,209 and 30,360 respectively)
Southland with Belgium	(31,195 and 30,280 respectively)

SKIP THE SELFIE, THEN?
11 AWFUL REVIEWS ON TRIP ADVISOR

◊ Otago Central Rail Trail: 'It was long and exceedingly boring'. (6 December 2010)

◊ Mt Eden, Auckland: 'Can't barely get to it for hordes of Asian tour buses parked willy nilly and disgorging their camera-totin' swarms all over the mountain like icing on a disgraced cake'. (11 November 2011)

◊ Auckland Domain: 'I guess it was the time of day, but they [sic] were very few animals to see. We searched and searched for the kiwis, but were unable to locate any at all'. (30 July 2013)

◊ Sky Tower, Auckland: 'All I remember is construction, massive plywood barriers everywhere we went, crushing masses of people, a feeling of utter chaos, disorganization, no helpful people, aaarrgghh'. (25 July 2016)

◊ Hobbiton: 'I felt the same way Elrond felt when Isildor decided to keep the ring in Mt Doom: hugely let down, slightly angry, and just peeved with myself for ever having faith in greedy men'. (29 April 2016)

◊ Te Papa Museum: 'It's certainly not a space where New Zealand history is allowed to awe you'. (29 May 2016)

◊ AJ Hackett Kawarau Bridge bungy jump: 'I felt that jumpers are treated like pigs that they just want to push out of the platform, rather than giving sufficient time to condition one's mind'. (14 December 2016)

◊ Polynesian Spa, Rotorua: 'The water in all pools were very dirty – so many bugs floating, there were many human body hair, many seagull feathers, etc. I understand that the thermal spa/hot springs will have some things in the water which may look like water is contaminated ... but what I found there were not natural'. (4 January 2017)

◊ Wai-O-Tapu Thermal Wonderland: 'Quite frankly I have seen more bubbles when my grandson farts in the bath'. (30 June 2017)

◊ Waitomo Glowworm Caves: '... it was pretty obvious that the glow worms in the cave were fake ...' (5 September 2017)

◊ Agrodome, Rotorua: 'During the shearing, the sheep had a bloody nose. The nursery and after-show visit of animals was challenging in that all the animals had some visible illnesses. Lambs in the nursery had diarrhea, one was limping painfully'. (9 September 2017)

It's not unusual: 12 ubiquitous street names (and how often they've been used)

◊ George Street   74

◊ Queen Street   69

◊ Beach Road   69

◊ High Street   68

◊ King Street   66

◊ Station Road   66

◊ Rata Street   57

◊ School Road   55

◊ Grey Street   54

◊ Church Street   52

◊ Elizabeth Street   52

◊ Victoria Street   50

Part of the family: 12 immigrants who've made a difference

◊ Farid Ahmed: A senior leader of the Dean's Avenue Mosque in Christchurch, he taught us a profound lesson in forgiveness when he publicly forgave the gunman who slaughtered his wife and 49 other members of the Muslim community on 15 March 2019. 'I don't hate him at all, not at all … I love him because he is human, he is a brother of mine,' he said. Born in Bangladesh.

◊ Joe Gock: In the 1960s, after black rot disease devastated the kumara crops grown on the Dargaville Flats, he assured the survival of the kumara supply when he gifted a disease-resistant strain from his market garden south of Auckland. Joe refused to take any payment and saw it as a way to repay his adoptive country. Born in China.

◊ Irene van Dyk: Quickly became the face of netball in New Zealand after her arrival in 2000, and 10 years later became the Silver Ferns most capped player. In 2010, she was flag bearer for the New Zealand team at the opening ceremony of the Commonwealth Games. Born in South Africa.

◊ Otto Groen: Spent seven years petitioning lawmakers to change the liquor licensing rules. The breweries, hotels, churches and the Salvation Army were all against him, but eventually, on 13 December 1961, Groen's Auckland restaurant became the first in New Zealand to be granted a liquor licence. Since then, restaurant diners have been allowed to enjoy a glass of wine with their meals and dining out is a far more civilized experience. Born in Holland.

◊ Roger Hall: Used theatre to point out the foibles and follies of middle New Zealand not only to Kiwis themselves but also to a highly amused global audience. His plays, which include *Glide Time, Middle-Age Spread and Four Flat Whites in Italy*, are performed and applauded worldwide. Born in England.

◊ Mitchell Pham: After fleeing his homeland in a boat with 67 other refugees, he spent 18 months in Indonesian refugee camps before arriving in New Zealand, alone, as a 14 year old. As an adult, he cofounded the Kiwi Connection Tech Hub, a platform used by NZ technology businesses to accelerate their presence in South East Asia. In July 2018, he became the first ethnic migrant/refugee to receive the World Class New Zealander Award. Born in Vietnam.

◊ Friedensreich Hundertwasser: Designer of toilets in Kawakawa, the Bay of Islands – the most photographed public convenience in New Zealand. Also, creator of the koru flag, the best-known design for an alternative New Zealand flag. Born in Austria.

◊ Ray Avery: As a boy living rough in London, he would seek warmth in libraries, where his fascination with science was sparked. He moved to New Zealand at the age of 14. In 2003, Avery founded Medicine Mondiale, which makes quality healthcare and equipment accessible to the world's poorest nations. Born in England.

◊ Ming-Jen Huang: Star of the 30 Second 'Spray and walk away' commercials. Huang, formerly a professional tour guide, dismissed complaints made to the Advertising Standards Authority, saying his performance as a Japanese professor with a bad accent didn't in any way disrespect the Asian community. 'The commercial is funny and it makes people happy', he wrote. 'What could possibly be wrong with that?' Born in Taiwan.

◊ Nándor Tánczos: The country's first Rastafarian MP began his maiden speech to Parliament in 1999 with greetings in the name of the Creator, the Most High Jah Ras Tafari. A strong advocate for cannabis law reform and direct-action protests, he later described his nine years in parliament as taking 'some of the polish off my soul'. Born in England to a Hungarian father and a mixed-race South African mother.

◊ Kim Dotcom: A self-described 'internet freedom fighter' who was granted residency in 2010 under the 'investor plus' category. In 2014, Dotcom founded the Internet Party, which then formed a political alliance with the Mana Party with great fanfare but little political traction. The High Court has ruled that Dotcom could be extradited to the United States to face criminal fraud charges. Born in Germany.

◊ Alex Gilbert: Adopted by his Kiwi parents when he was two years old. In 2013, he started using social media to locate his parents and succeeded after a quick search. In 2015, he started the organisation I'm Adopted, which has helped hundreds of people around the world trace their birth families in Russia. Born in Russia.

8 STRANGE AND REMARKABLE FACTS ABOUT BLUFF

◊ You can't count on a late night out in Bluff. At the Oyster Cove Restaurant and Bar, the latest that meal orders are accepted is 7.30 pm.

◊ For nearly 60 years, the international signpost at Stirling Point was wildly inaccurate and the source of much tourist bemusement because the markers for Cape Reinga and Wellington (both north) faced in completely opposite directions. The egregious error wasn't corrected until late 2018.

◊ Room 2 of the Foveaux Hotel is said to be haunted. The ghost is thought to be that of Mary Cameron, the original owner of the Temperance Boarding House, which was demolished in 1937 to make way for the Foveaux Hotel.

◊ Bluff is not the farthest you can get from the Equator, because Bluff is approximately 400 km closer to the Equator than Land's End in the UK is.

◊ Andy Haden, old-time talent agent, is an honorary citizen in recognition of his heroic oyster-eating attempt during the Bluff Rugby Club's centennial celebrations in 1989. In front of 500 witnesses, he downed 18.5 dozen oysters (222 oysters, to be precise) – until, as one journalist stated, 'his sense of wellness deserted him'.

◊ Cilla McQueen, New Zealand Poet Laureate for 2009–2011, is a resident. She penned the words 'Beneath the sea the oysters rock gently in their beds' to accompany a mosaic mural that formed part of an urban rejuvenation project.

◇ In October 2017, broadcaster Marcus Lush stated during one of his night-time radio shows that, because he doesn't own such an appliance, he will occasionally avail himself of the clothes drier at the camping ground close to his home.

◇ Victor Manson Spencer, from Bluff, was one of 28 New Zealand servicemen court-martialled and sentenced to death for desertion during the First World War. As he stood before the firing squad on 24 February 1918, his last words were 'Are you there, Padre?' The parson replied, 'I'm here, lad'. Spencer was then summarily shot. In 2000, Spencer was officially pardoned under the provisions of the Pardon for Soldiers of the Great War Act.

---

8 TOWN SLOGANS BEST FORGOTTEN

◇ Dannevirke: Take a Liking to a Viking

◇ Gore: World Capital of Brown Trout Fishing

◇ Matamata: The Town That's Racing Ahead

◇ Naseby: 2000 ft above Worry Level

◇ Porirua: P-Town

◇ Te Puke: Stop and Taste Te Puke

◇ The Hutt Valley: Right up My Hutt Valley

◇ Tuatapere: New Zealand's Sausage Capital

21 WORDS — OR IS IT A POEM? — THAT YOU CAN MAKE FROM THE LETTERS IN 'MIKE HOSKING'

gosh	hongi
ego	hikoi
gnome	kinks
oinks	noise
honks	omens
neighs	sheik
eskimo	skink
monkish	snog
smoking	singe
gismo	sigh
gonk	

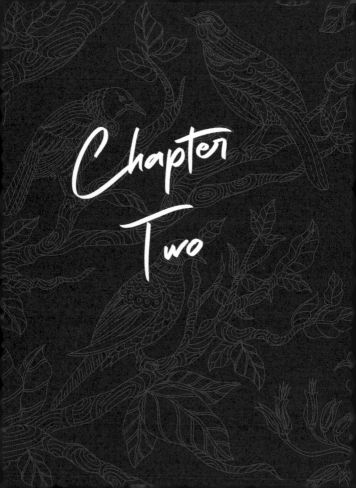

Chapter

Two

LOVE, LIFE and the KIDS:

Family Circles

DAYS THAT CHANGED NEW ZEALAND

19 August 2013: Same-sex marriage is legalized

Two days ago, on 17 August, the bill passed its final reading by 77 votes to 44. Cheers from the public galleries rang out and the sound of 'Pokarekare Ana' resonated around the chamber. Finally, a fair go attitude had prevailed. From today, 48 hours later, same-sex couples can legally marry. Love is love, and there is nothing to fear by sanctioning it with a marriage ceremony. New Zealand becomes the first country in Oceania, the fourth in the Southern Hemisphere, and the fifteenth overall to allow same-sex couples to marry. It's a quiet revolution, but it is progress.

---

5 NICHE DATING SITES WHERE KIWIS LOOK FOR LOVE

Singles Over Sixty: Where maturity matters. www.singlesover60.co.nz

Hookup & Casual Dating: Appealing to commitment-phobes, though a testimonial on the website insists the couple were so well suited they are now living together. www.hudapp.com

Academic Singles: A no-brainer, really. No, wait … www.academicsingles.co.nz

---

We Love Dates: Avoid the mainstream and look for love with punks, goths, metal-heads, rockers or emos instead. By the look of things, piercings and tattoos are pretty much compulsory. www.welovedates.com/nz/alternative-dating

My Sugar: Where rich meets beautiful and nobody is fooling anybody that attraction is based on love. http://www.mysugar.co.nz/

How 10 prominent Kiwi couples met

Prime Minister Jacinda Ardern and Clarke Gayford: Concerned about the potential ramifications of the GCSB Amendment Bill, Clarke expressed his views in writing to National MP Nikki Kaye. She didn't respond, so he addressed his concerns to Jacinda instead. They met for coffee to talk things over – and one thing led to another.

Celebrity chef Nadia Lim and Carlos Bagrie: The couple met in Dunedin's legendary Captain Cook Tavern during Orientation Week at Otago University. Nadia was there to study nutrition and dietetics and Carlos was doing marketing and psychology. 'I was looking around and there was this beautiful girl smiling at me,' says Carlos, 'so I went over and we started talking'. They've been talking ever since. 'When I first met him,' says Nadia, 'he was shocking. He could barely boil an egg.'

Political editor Jessica Mutch and Iain McKay: She worked as a reporter in Wellington and would have seen him, a prime ministerial bodyguard, standing on the other side of John Key during stand-up interviews at the Beehive, but the two never spoke. It wasn't until 2015, a few months before Jessica was due to leave her role as TVNZ's Europe correspondent, that Iain saw her on TV and sent her a friend request on Facebook. Soon, they were Skyping on a daily basis and eventually met for a first date in Paris.

All Black Richie McCaw and Black Stick Gemma Flynn: The rugby legend messaged hockey player Gemma Flynn on Facebook to commiserate over the loss of a big game, saying he knew exactly what it felt like to lose an important match. Apparently not bothered so much – or maybe because she was on tour and distracted – Gemma forgot about the message for two weeks before eventually replying. The pair wed in January 2017 and now have a baby daughter.

Politician Grant Robertson and Alf Kaiwai: Met when they were both playing for the country's first gay rugby team, the Krazy Knights. In his maiden speech in Parliament, Robertson noted, 'I was the number eight and he was the halfback.' After ten years together, they married in a civil union in 2009.

Singer-songwriter Ladyhawke (Pip Brown) and actress Madeleine Sami: First met at the 2009 New Zealand Music Awards. Stars collided, so to speak, when they were introduced by Kiwi actress Lucy Lawless. Brown and Sami married in January 2015 in a private ceremony and welcomed a baby daughter in October 2017.

Meteorologist Dan Corbett and Helen: He predicted a change in 1997 when they both worked at the BBC in London. Helen worked in the make-up department and Dan was a new weatherman who flirted successfully while getting his face powdered.

Stand-up comedian Nick Rado and yoga instructor Sophie Rimmer: Met at the Classic Comedy Bar in Auckland. He was MC-ing a gig; she was in the audience. She laughed at his jokes, and somehow, phone numbers were exchanged. They married in 2014 and now have a son and a daughter.

Broadcaster and writer Tim Wilson and Rachel Schryvers: Met at church. Although Tim was raised Presbyterian, he started going to mass and was received into the Roman Catholic Church in 2012. He spotted Rachel across the pews at Auckland's St Patrick's Cathedral. The couple now have three young sons.

Magician Andre Vegas and ballerina Adriana: Adriana Harper had been a dancer with the Royal NZ Ballet for almost 11 years when she left in 2015. Full-day rehearsals, five or six days a week, interspersed with intensive performing and touring had taken a toll, physically and mentally. Knowing her career as a professional ballet dancer was finished but not knowing what to do next, she picked up the phone to call her friend Andre, a magician and illusionist, to see if he needed an assistant. He did. They began performing together, love blossomed, and they married in June 2016.

---

7 DISASTROUS LOVE STORIES IMMORTALIZED IN POETRY

The Poets, by Iain Sharp ('How could I drive her to grasp at me and gasp "Kiss me forever, you spectacular hunk of virile brawn"???')

Having Already Walked Out on Everyone I Ever Said I Loved, by Hera Lindsay Bird ('The official theme of this poem is / The official theme of all my poems which is / You get in love and then you die')

Proposal at Allens Beach, by Iain Lonie ('I can't promise much / but you won't forget having been here / nor who you came with, and all / that followed, if it followed.')

Advice to a Discarded Lover, by Fleur Adcock ('In you / I see maggots close to the surface. / You are eaten up by self-pity, / Crawling with unlovable pathos.')

Catastrophes as Only the Thin Know Them, by Anthony McCarten ('Moments pass, and then there is a loud knock at the door. / There is nothing else I can do / And I open it / And it's everyone but the one / I'd most wanted to see.')

Wedding Party and After, by Sam Hunt ('One woman got so drunk she pulled / her husband's pants down yelling, *Look at this I've got / to fucking live with it!'*)

Dear Sir, by Kate Camp ('This correspondence is now closed.')

BEST MONTH TO
GIVE BIRTH TO A SPORTS STAR

To maximize your child's chance of hallowed-sports-star status, bless them with a May birthday. More inductees in the New Zealand Sports Hall of Fame have been born in that month than any other. If born in May, your budding sports star will share the month with these Kiwi legends:

1 May	Dave Gerrard: an Olympic swimmer who became a sports administrator and sports medicine specialist.
7 May	Stacey Jones: rugby league footballer, among the greatest this country has produced.
9 May	Lesley Rumball: netballer who played for the Silver Ferns from 1993 to 2005.
12 May	Stan Lay: Olympic and Empire Games javelin thrower who, at the 1950 Empire Games, took the oath on behalf of all competitors.
18 May	Tom Heeney: professional heavyweight boxer, best remembered for challenging Gene Tunney for the heavyweight championship of the world in New York City on 26 July 1928.
23 May	Erin Baker: a triathlete who won numerous world championship and Ironman titles.
23 May	Billy Savidan: long distance runner who, at the 1930 British Empire Games, won the six-mile race despite pulling up early, not realizing there was one more lap to run.

24 May	Ian Kirkpatrick: All Blacks captain from 1972 to 1974.
26 May	Bob Fitzsimmons: the sport of boxing's first three-division world champion.
26 May	Glenn Turner: began his Test cricketing career with a duck, but evolved into one of the country's best batsmen.
28 May	Bill Baillie: long-distance runner, who represented New Zealand at the 1964 Summer Olympics in Tokyo, where he placed sixth in the 5000 m.
30 May	Allison Roe: in 1981, won both the Boston Marathon and New York City Marathon, becoming the second of only two women to accomplish the feat in the same year.

8 Kiwi lads who followed in their famous father's footsteps

Otis Frizzell, artist (son of Dick Frizzell)

Sam Morgan, philanthropist (son of Gareth Morgan)

Peter Hillary, mountaineer and philanthropist (son of Sir Ed Hillary)

Anton Oliver, All Blacks captain (son of Frank Oliver)

Andrew Kerr, cardiologist (son of Alan Kerr)

Phillip Mills, athlete and businessman (son of Les Mills)

Richard Hadlee, cricketer (son of Walter Hadlee)

John Kirk, politician (son of Norman Kirk)

... and 3 who didn't

Grayson Coutts, make-up artist (son of Russell Coutts, professional sailor and five-times winner of the America's Cup)

Sam Mahon, artist and writer (son of Peter Mahon, High Court judge best known for his Commission of Inquiry into the Mount Erebus disaster)

Robert Weeks, principal bassoonist in the New Zealand Symphony Orchestra (son of Roger Harman Weeks, orthopedic surgeon and prominent Freemason)

---

15 BABY NAMES THAT MIGHT BE OKAY IN AUSTRALIA BUT NOT IN NEW ZEALAND

Banjo	Diamantina
Kylie	Sybilla
Shane	Raelene
Clancy	Jannali
Sheila	Gough
Adelaide	Drover
Dusty	Murray
Jarrah	

THE 10 BEST NAMES FROM GLORIAVALE

According to *What We Believe*, a booklet summarising the doctrines of the Gloriavale Christian Community, 'Names should not just be pretty sounds with no apparent meaning, nor should they be names taken in honour of worldly relatives or film stars.' Meaningful names of community members (past and present) occasionally include idiosyncratic spellings:

◊ Dove Love

◊ Constance Ready

◊ Fervent Stedfast

◊ Harmony Helpful

◊ Hopeful Christian

◊ Paradise Courage

◊ Prayer Darling

◊ Promise Overcomer

◊ Purity Valor

◊ Trusty Disciple.

---

5 Kiwi blokes who've cried in public

◊ Rugby icon Jonah Lomu: became emotional when interviewed by Paul Holmes, as he described his sadness at the fact that his mother was not present when he married his first wife, Tanya Rutter, in 1996.

◊ Broadcaster Mike Hosking: choked up at the end of his final *Seven Sharp* episode in 2017 as he talked about how much he was looking forward to having more time to spend with his family.

◊ All Blacks halfback Aaron Smith: wept when he made a public apology for his airport indiscretion in 2016.

◊ Comedian Jono Pryor: broke down on air while paying tribute to a close friend who had taken his own life in 2017.

◊ Broadcaster John Campbell: erupted in tears during his Campbell Live TV programme in 2015 when American singer-songwriter Sharon Van Etten made a surprise appearance. Reporter Ali Ikram had organized for Van Etten to sing for Campbell during a live cross from the King's Arms because Campbell, a huge fan, had been forced to miss her concert.

---

5 PICTURESQUE PLACES FOR A PARK-UP, FROM AN EXPERIENCED PASH-UP ARTIST

Love is not always totally blind. Conducive surroundings are crucial if you want to elevate a quick snog to a lingering and luxurious session of lip-locking. The adviser for this list has travelled the length of New Zealand, appraising the scenery for the most environmentally friendly backdrops to a backseat tryst. These are her top recommendations.

◊ The foreshore of French Pass Village, which overlooks D'Urville Island in the Marlborough Sounds

◊ Buffalo Beach, the main beach for Whitianga

◊ The grassy bank of the stunning tidal Whananaki Estuary, Northland

◊ Virginia Lake, in the city of Whanganui

◊ Palliser Bay, characterized by rumbustious seas and bracing winds, on the northern shore of Cook Strait.

…and the worst in-car snog ever

After dinner one evening in March 2016, Simon Hartnoll and his girlfriend returned to their vehicle in a car park building in Newmarket, Auckland. While exiting the building, Hartnoll stopped the car and put the handbrake on, but left the gear in drive as he leant in towards his date. Both unbuckled their seatbelts. As Hartnoll manoeuvred himself into position for a snog, he hit the accelerator pedal. The car shot forward, crashed through a barrier and plunged 14 metres into the street below. Hartnoll suffered rib and clavicle fractures as well as spinal injuries. His date suffered serious head injuries. The relationship did not survive, and Hartnoll was eventually found guilty of careless driving causing injury.

LUST AND LONGING:
8 BITS OF RELATIONSHIP ADVICE THAT HAVEN'T AGED WELL

Playdate, the country's first music, art, fashion, and lifestyle magazine was published between 1960 and 1972. Aimed at 'teens to twenty-sixers', the magazine devoted pages of advice each issue to lovelorn, angst-ridden readers in a section called 'Dear Sheba'. Let's just say it was another era ...

◊ 'Boys might whistle and stare because they know it worries you. If you *completely* ignore them, they may stop. But really it isn't so terrible – you ought to feel flattered – they're not doing any harm.'

◊ 'You must help yourself all you can in order to find a boyfriend. First of all, do you always look clean and neat, your hair nicely done, your clothes in good order? Always look your best, and be friendly and cheerful.'

◊ 'Next time he gets in a temper and then asks to be forgiven, do not forgive him too easily – let him wait a while. Maybe a fright will make him more careful.'

◊ 'All you should do towards getting married is to concentrate on growing up sensibly. If you're working, try to save money; if you sew or knit, you could make things for your box.'

◊ 'It wouldn't hurt at all to tell your friends beforehand that your Dad didn't like smoking and would they please refrain. They won't laugh at you - they'll respect you for wanting to abide by your parents' wishes.'

◊ 'There's nothing silly about remembering a friend on a birthday. If the friend likes reading, a book is suitable - or a handkerchief - or a ballpoint pen - or, if he has a particular hobby, something useful regarding it.'

◊ 'Ask at your public library about books on sex education. (If you're too shy to ask, telephone and ask for the name of books and then just look at them yourself on the shelves - or do exactly the same in a bookstore.)'

◊ 'If you would only stop taking every boy so seriously, you'd be much happier. Just because you went out with another boy didn't mean you had to tell you boyfriend you were through. There's room in teenagers' hearts for several boys at once and going steady is just asking for trouble.'

7 Kiwi dropouts whose parents needn't have worried

Educational crash-and-burn doesn't mean success will forever elude you. Until they found their true calling, these academically uncommitted students would undoubtedly have caused their parents some angst.

◊ Rob Ewen: during his second year of business studies at AUT, Rob decided to drop out and set up his own business selling t-shirts printed with images of iconic kiwiana. His Mr Vintage collection, designed to be a record of New Zealand's pop culture, has included a 'Nek Minnit' t-shirt and one emblazoned with 'Keep Calm, Piri's On'. When Jacinda became prime minister, he added a 'Let's Do This' jute tote bag to his range.

◊ Wira Gardiner: reliably came bottom of his class at Whakatane High School. Fifty years later, he founded and headed the Waitangi Tribunal, as well as Te Puni Kokiri (the Ministry of Maori Development). He has credited his skilful public service and business success to what he learned from 20 years in the army. In 2008, he was made a Knight of the New Zealand Order of Merit for his services to Maori.

◊ Bryan Old: severely dyslexic, Bryan Old hated everything about school and admits he always asked his wife to sign cheques for him. As a McDonald's franchisee, however, he was a roaring success. After Kiwis had been putting up with the American version of a burger for 15 years, Old managed to persuade management to introduce a burger that accommodated a slab of cold beetroot and a greasy fried egg on top of the meat patty. The Kiwi Burger was born, and the national palate has never looked back. Neither has Bryan Old's bank balance.

◊ Dan Bidois: after dropping out of high school in Auckland, he then survived cancer treatment before settling into a job as a butcher's apprentice. With encouragement, he decided he needed further study. In 2010, at the age of 27, he beat two thousand other applicants worldwide to win a Fulbright Scholarship and completed a two-year master's in public policy at Harvard.

◊ Andy Davies: was asked to leave the decile-10 St Kentigern College in Auckland when he was 15. He is now one of New Zealand's biggest private property developers, buying up, doing up and selling up commercial and residential properties. He is now worth over $75 million. His most well-known project is Ponsonby Central, a complex accommodating chic retail an d food outlets.

◊ Graeme Hart: left school at 16 and worked as a tow-truck driver and a panel beater. He later completed an MBA at Otago University. For a thesis topic, he wrote about using leveraged buyouts to acquire under-performing companies that produced everyday items; he then went on to buy and merge four party-hire companies. Before long, he had an exclusive grasp on the provision of goods and services for corporate events and, by 2019, his net worth had risen to over $10 billion. That's *billion*, not million.

◊ Parris Goebel: a self-taught hip hop dancer, Parris dropped out of Auckland Girls' Grammar early to concentrate on her dancing and ended up being named Young New Zealander of the Year in 2014. As a choreographer, she has worked for Little Mix, Justin Bieber, Rihanna, Janet Jackson, Jennifer Lopez and Nicki Minaj, and in 2016 she won Female Choreographer of the Year and Live Performance of the Year at the World Of Dance Awards.

ACADEMICALLY ASTONISHING:
7 KIWIS WITH HONORARY DOCTORATES
FROM WAIKATO UNIVERSITY

2000	Neil Finn, singer-songwriter
2001	Tim Finn, singer-songwriter
2006	Howard Morrison, singer and entertainer
2008	Ruud Kleinpaste, naturalist
2011	Jools Topp, singer-songwriter
2011	Lynda Topp, singer-songwriter
2013	Susan Devoy, former professional squash player and Race Relations Commissioner

... and 14 illustrious alumni with honorary doctorates from elsewhere

◊ Queen Elizabeth, The Queen Mother (in 1966, from the University of Auckland)

◊ Rewi Alley (in 1972, from Victoria University of Wellington)

◊ Lloyd Geering (in 1976, from the University of Otago)

◊ Charles, Prince of Wales (in 1981, from the University of Otago)

◊ Alison Holst (in 1997, from the University of Otago)

◊ Sir Peter Blake (in 1999, from Massey University)

- ◊ Aung San Suu Kyi (in 1999, from Victoria University of Wellington)

- ◊ Sam Neill (in 2002, from the University of Canterbury)

- ◊ John Clarke, aka Fred Dagg (in 2007, from Victoria University of Wellington)

- ◊ Bob Charles (in 2007, from Lincoln University)

- ◊ Richie McCaw (in 2012, from Lincoln University)

- ◊ Graham Henry (in 2012, from the University of Canterbury)

- ◊ Rob Fyfe (in 2015, from the University of Canterbury)

- ◊ Marti Friedlander (in 2016, from the University of Auckland)

Chapter Three

FOOD and DRINK:

On the Table

---

2 December 1917: End of the 6 o'clock swill

The government has bowed to public pressure and held a referendum on abolishing an archaic licensing law that insists pub doors are closed at six o'clock each evening. For 50 years, men have crowded into pubs after work to get as much beer on board as possible before the doors shut at 6 pm. Today marks the end of the infamous '6 o'clock swill'. It is a defining moment in the country's social history. From now on, the way Kiwis drink and socialize is changed for good.

---

10 KIWIS OTHER KIWIS WOULD LIKE TO INVITE TO THEIR NEXT BARBECUE

◊ Anika Moa (to lead the sing-along around the fire)

◊ Richie McCaw (for a nostalgic chat about the golden days of the Rugby World Cup)

◊ Dariush Lolaiy, chef of Auckland's Cazador game restaurant (who can make award-winning dishes from anything you catch in the wild, and even whip up a pig-face salad, if needed)

◊ Sir Peter Leitch, aka The Mad Butcher (bound to bring along a few sausages)

◊ Sam Neill (likely to bring some of his own wine)

◊ Taiki Waititi (for pure entertainment)

◊ Winston Peters (for the sake of argument)

◊ Mike King (to ensure everyone feels okay)

◊ John Campbell (who will repeatedly declare everything to be 'Marvellous!')

◊ Rena Owen (if the barbecue runs out of gas, she could always cook the men some eggs)

…and 7 who are likely to be left off the invite list…

◊ Len Brown, former mayor of Auckland (because it's hard to swallow and visualize the Ngati Whatua Room at the same time)

◊ Aaron Gilmore (who may not yet have learned the art of self-service and could sit back and imperiously order extra wine)

◊ Mark Lundy (in case he spills something indeterminate on his shirtfront)

◊ Ewen McDonald (acquitted of murdering Feilding farmer Scott Guy, but nevertheless his treatment of livestock indicated despicable meat-handling skills)

◊ Julia Clements (president of the NZ Vegetarian Society, who would probably frown a lot at the sight of animal blood)

◊ Mike Tomlinson (chairman of the Heart Foundation)

◊ Lauraine Jacobs (former food editor of *Cuisine* magazine, who might not have a kind word to say)

6 DECADES OF KIWI FOOD FASHIONS

◊ The 60s: Chicken-in-a-basket; dehydrated Surprise peas; salad dressing made with sweetened condensed milk diluted with vinegar; French onion soup dip; prawn cocktail. Popular cookbook: *Triple Tested Recipe Book,* by Thelma Christie for the Lower Hutt Plunket Society (1959)

◊ The 70s: Fondues; quiche; Wiener schnitzel; surf'n'turf; pâté and garlic bread; carrot cake. Popular cookbooks: *Food Without Fuss,* by Alison Holst (1972); *Food for Flatters,* by Michael Volkerling (1973)

◊ The 80s: Homemade muesli bars; orange roughy; microwave cookery; Moët (ubiquitously mispronounced as Mo-ay); ratatouille; hummus; pesto. Popular cookbooks: *A Vegetable Cookbook,* by Digby Law (1982); *The New Zealand Microwave Cookbook,* by Jan Bilton (1984)

◊ The 90s: Caesar salad; pasta; sundried tomatoes; red wine jus; BLATs on toasted white bread; balsamic drizzle; nachos. Popular cookbook: *Marvellous Muffins,* by Alison Holst (1994)

◊ The 00s: Eggplant and zucchini served in stacks; sushi; paninis; bowl lattes. Popular cookbook: *Food in a Minute Favourites*: *Celebrating 10 years,* by Allyson Gofton (2006)

◊ The 10s: Quinoa salad; pork banh mi; foam; kale; smashed avo; ramen noodles; green smoothies; turmeric lattes; kimchi, kombucha, flaxseed crackers; cronuts. Popular cookbook: *Coming Unstuck,* by Sarah Tuck (published in 2017)

5 SAD-ARSE DINNERS FROM
SARAH TUCK FOR A NIGHT IN WITH NETFLIX

Sarah Tuck road-tested these recipes through the course of a long heartbreak. Her book, *Coming Unstuck*, carried a persuasive message of food-as-therapy when times are bad. She speaks from experience when she says that, on nights when it's just you and Netflix, there's comfort in a meal for one, matched to the movie on screen.

◊ Gourmet mac 'n' cheese for one: pan-fried pancetta and sweet, slow cooked onions folded through a cheese sauce spiked with gruyere and parmesan. The whole thing is topped with ciabatta cubes, buttered with a little garlic butter and a little more cheese. (Great for US shows like *House of Cards*.)

◊ 10-minute pizza: a thin pizza base with tomato paste, loaded with parmesan, grated mozzarella, prosciutto and torn buffalo. (Good for eating while watching *The Talented Mr Ripley*.)

◊ The ultimate gourmet toastie: two slices of grainy wholewheat bread fried in butter and slathered with American mustard, then loaded up with caramelized onions, pastrami or corned beef slices, Swiss cheese and sliced gherkins. (Great for any US show – *Breaking Bad, Orange is the New Black*, even *Mad Men*...)

◊ Perfect scrambled eggs: three eggs whisked with a tablespoon or two of cream and heated gently over melted butter in a frying pan. Served on toast: sometimes it's a wholegrain kind of night; others, thickly sliced ciabatta; and sometimes, a couple of slices of buttered white toast. (Theme match this with *The Crown* or *Peaky Blinders*.)

◊ Quick green soup: soften onion in a little olive oil over a low heat, add chicken or vegetable stock and bring to a boil. Throw in a small finely chopped spud and a couple of cloves of garlic, cook for 5 minutes then add chopped broccoli florets, a vast handful of spinach, a small chopped zucchini and some peas. Cook for another 10 minutes then add some fresh basil and mint leaves. Remove from the heat, blend with a whiz stick and then serve with a dollop of Greek yoghurt and plenty of sea salt and black pepper ... and dukkah, if you keep a stash in the cupboard. (If you're watching a lot of hot bods on the screen, this is the healthy indulgent dinner.)

Source: Sarah Tuck, author of *Coming Unstuck: Recipes to Get You Back on Track*

---

12 Kiwi classics you're going to miss if you go vegan

◊ Bluff oysters

◊ Vogel's bread

◊ Whitebait fritters

◊ Fish and chips

◊ Steak'n'cheese pie

◊ Roast lamb

◊ Pavlova

◊ Griffin's gingernuts

◊ Hokey-pokey ice cream

◊ Chocolate fish

◊ Whittaker's peanut slabs

◊ Manuka honey

8 DISHES FROM THE HOKITIKA WILD FOODS FESTIVAL THAT ARE UNLIKELY TO FEATURE AT YOUR NEXT DINNER PARTY

◊ Huhu grubs

◊ Duck heads

◊ Crocodile bites

◊ Fish eyes

◊ Scorpions

◊ Pork blood casserole

◊ Worms

◊ Deep-fried pig's ears

8 FOOD ITEMS TO SEND AS CHRISTMAS GIFTS TO KIWI KIDS OVERSEAS

◊ Pic's pinati pata (peanut butter)

◊ Whittaker's peanut slabs

◊ Wattie's tomato sauce

◊ Jaffas

◊ Chocolate fish

◊ Pohutukawa honey

◊ Marmite

◊ Healtheries feijoa teabags

More beersies for you: 16 New Zealand boutique beers with odd names

Liberty Brewing Company Knife Party IPA

Parrotdog Dead Canary Pale Ale

Three Boys Hoppy Porter

Weezledog Easy Weezy NZ Session IPA

Yeastie Boys Pot Kettle Black South Pacific Porter

8 Wired Hopwired IPA

Behemoth C's Get Degrees Old School West Coast IPA

8 Wired Semi Conductor Session IPA

Behemoth Hopped Up on Pils

Croucher Lowrider A Very Small IPA

Behemoth Brave Bikkie Brown Ale

Epic Hop Zombie Double IPA

Garage Project Fuzz Box Fuzzy Pale Ale

Deep Creek's Pontoon in a Monsoon IPA

Kereru's For Great Justice Wood-Fired Toasted Coconut Porter

Emerson's Bookbinder

8 RECIPES IN FOOD FOR FLATTERS THAT UNIVERSITY STUDENTS REJECT

◊ Veggie cheese rice cakes: Arborio rice - are you serious?

◊ Strawberry shortcakes: Sounds suspiciously 50s.

◊ Chinese chews: Does Meng Foon, our race relations commissioner, know about these?

◊ Cheese ball: Is this still a thing?

◊ Blue cheese spread: Don't want to jeopardize my chances later.

◊ Salmon fillets with teriyaki sauce: My student loan only stretches so far.

◊ Scallops mornay: Nah, fish and chips are easier.

◊ Wholemeal bread: Nothing comes between me and my Vogel's.

7 FAST-FOOD ITEMS WITH FRIGHTENING KILOJOULE COUNTS

If you don't want to feel bad about your fast-food indulgences, look away now.

Wendy's	Baconator mushroom melt burger	4400 kJ
Macdonald's	Gourmet homestyle Angus burger	3520 kJ
KFC	Colonel's stack zinger burger	3631 kJ
Pizza Hut	2 slices extra-large stuffed crust BBQ meat supreme pizza	3372 kJ

Subway	Chicken and bacon ranch melt 6-inch sandwich	2090 kJ
Mexicali Fresh	Supreme nachos	6550 kJ
Burger King	Angus steakhouse with streaky bacon	3506 kJ

---

10 TAKEAWAY FOODS
WITH BIG PRICE JUMPS FROM 2009 TO 2019

A cake or biscuit	43%	(From $2.98 to $4.27)
A cookie	41%	(From $1.57 to $2.21)
A hot meat pie	38%	(From $3.14 to $4.34)
A muffin	35%	(From $2.82 to $3.80)
Fish and chips	30%	(From $5.26 to $6.83)
A cup of tea	29%	(From 2.65 to $3.43)
A toasted sandwich	26%	(From $3.77 to $4.74)
Soft drink, 1.5 litres	24%	(From $2.15 to $2.67)
A cup of coffee	21%	(From $3.19 to $3.87)
Fried chicken, 5 pieces	21%	(From $10.13 to 12.26)

Source: Department of Statistics Food Price Index

INDIGESTIBLE: 8 BAD-TASTE LISTINGS ON BAMBOOZLE RESTAURANT'S MENU

The menu, widely rejected as 'tone deaf' and 'juvenile racist trash', is now permanently out of circulation since chef Phillip Kraal closed the restaurant's doors for good in January 2019. Kraal had earlier defended his menu as 'a hit with the customers', but eventually admitted on Facebook that the Christchurch restaurant was experiencing challenges that were 'simply overwhelming'. We're not sad.

◊ Ho Lee Kok: Cook Island marinated fish salad wrapped in warm roti with crisp salad greens

◊ Suk Sum Teet: fried spicy rice salad larb gai

◊ Yum Ee Kouw Patt: fried tofu and shitake mushrooms with garlic and spring onion in warm roti

◊ Eja Ku Rait: fried garlic chicken knuckles with chilled cucumber and mint wrapped in warm roti

◊ Rital Phatt Ee: char siu style braised pork shoulder with a sweet, sour, ginger glaze in warm roti

◊ Vaag Yoo Owl Brown: Bamboozle's twist on the 'slider', a food trend popularized by Al Brown

◊ Gayeddie Crystal Dumprings: assorted Asian mushrooms and root vegetables steamed in transparent pastry

◊ Me Fa Canarde: charred sweet, sticky, spicy duck wings with cocaine mayo dipping sauce

7 UNEXPECTED USES FOR A
DECOMMISSIONED SUPERMARKET TROLLEY

Supermarket trolleys cost Countdown between $100 and $135 each, depending on size, and Malcolm Stewart, the National Refit Manager for Countdown, says that the supermarket chain has to replace between 8000 and 10,000 of them each year.

The trolleys that end up in creeks and riverbeds (or even in people's homes) represent a lot of recycling that could have happened. Just because the wheels get jammed and it can't make it smoothly down the shopping aisle in a straight line without squeaking, there is no reason not to love and appreciate the supermarket trolley beyond its value as scrap metal. Consider the possibilities for its reincarnation as:

◊ A crayfish basket

◊ A modern art installation

◊ A bird cage or chicken coop

◊ A trailer to tow behind a bike

◊ A rolling storage rack in the kitchen

◊ A portable planting box (when filled with sphagnum moss)

◊ An armchair (when bent into shape and supplied with enough cushions).

Cooking lessons:
11 reasons it's a miracle Air New Zealand earns any compliments for its in-flight meals

On the ground, quality and presentation are relatively straightforward matters. Airline chefs have additional worries, having to consider the effect of altitude, reheating, safety practices, and even the amount of time that the food needs to be held.

◊ Flying does terrible things to passengers' taste buds. The lack of humidity dries the nose, making it harder to enjoy the aroma of food, and the lack of cabin pressure numbs taste buds. This means it is harder to perceive saltiness and sweetness.

◊ Sour flavours, such as vinegar or lemon juice, are roughly 30 per cent stronger in the air, so salad dressings need to have their acidity reduced.

◊ Herbs can be problematic. Dried herbs don't work well, so fresh herbs are used wherever possible. However, many also taste quite different on the palate of an airline passenger. Rosemary, for example, starts tasting like hay. Herbs such as basil, chives and parsley release less flavour under the lower air pressures, so need to be used in double quantities.

◊ Reheating fish produces unpleasant an aroma. Clever airline cooks create a potato crust to boost flavour and stop the smell of the fish permeating the whole cabin.

◊ Passengers with numb taste buds will enjoy spicy curries and more robust wines, because strong flavours can survive the on-board conditions. Tomato juice is much more popular in the sky than on the ground.

◊ Planes don't generally have microwaves, so food must be reheated in a convection oven.

◊ Mass food poisoning among passengers would be disastrous, so food safety is a primary concern. In 1992, on an Aerolineas Argentinas flight from Buenos Aires to Los Angeles, 76 passengers got sick from eating cholera-tainted shrimp, and an elderly passenger died.

◊ Bananas, despite their popularity with children, are off the menu, because bananas go brown and mushy when refrigerated.

◊ Menus must be changed every couple of months to prevent boredom in frequent flyers.

◊ Menus should reflect the destination being served and the time of day of the flight.

◊ Meals must be meticulously costed. (American Airlines reportedly saved US$40,000 in a year by serving one less olive in each salad.)

SWEET AS? 4 DESCRIPTIONS OF CLASSIC KIWI DELICACIES

◊ Mutton bird: 'If correctly cooked, it tastes like a kipper – if badly cooked, like nothing on earth'. *From N to Z,* by Carl V Smith (1947)

◊ Oysters: 'The Astrolabe oyster, found as its name implies at Astrolabe, near Nelson, is a fine large fat oyster when in good condition, but rather too coppery in flavour to be eaten *au naturel;* cooked, however, it is excellent, and if kept for a time and fed, it loses much of the unpleasant metallic twang …' Isobel Broad in *New Zealand Exhibition Cookery Book* (1889)

◊ Meat pies: 'Three o'clock in the morning, you're buying a pie from the BP station, what must you always do? That pie's probably been in the warming drawer for about 12 hours. It will be thermo-nuclear. You must always blow on the pie. Safer communities together, okay?' Police Officer Glen on *Police Ten 7* (2009)

◊ Chocolate raspberry pavlova: 'The crisp and chewy chocolate meringue base, rich in cocoa and beaded nuggets of chopped plain chocolate, provides a sombre, almost purple-brown layer beneath the fat whiteness of the cream and matt, glowering crimson raspberries on top: it is a killer combination.' Nigella Lawson, in *Nigella Summer* (2002)

Gone? Maybe, maybe not:
5 fabulous facts about Girl Guide biscuits

March and April will never be quite the same, now that Girl Guide biscuits have gone the way of the moa. For over 60 years, the Guides would set up their stalls, raising funds through sales of a quality product beloved by the nation. In 2018, it was decided that Guides would focus more on their core purpose and programmes, and, in March 2019, the last packet of biscuits was sold – at least, that's how it seemed, until October 2019, when Griffins biscuit company came to the rescue and, on a trial basis, made the biscuits available again through supermarkets, with $1 from every packet sold going to Girl Guiding NZ.

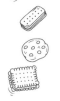

◊ Girl Guide biscuits were a major annual fundraiser for over 60 years.

◊ The recipe never changed from the time the biscuits first went on sale in 1957.

◊ The biscuits were a key ingredient in excellent lemon cheesecake, chocolate rum truffles, and rocky road slice.

◊ Over the years, new varieties were added, such as the chocolate and mini varieties.

◊ The selling drive was easily the largest girl-led business in New Zealand.

---

7 FOREIGN ITEMS FOUND IN FOOD BY PUBLIC HEALTH INSPECTORS

◊ A weta at the base of an ice-cream cone

◊ A shotgun pellet in beef steak

◊ A cockroach in a takeaway meal

◊ A black widow spider in a bunch of Californian grapes

◊ A $2 note in a full bottle of milk, in the days when a pint cost only four cents

◊ A mouse inside a loaf of bread (the mouse had been surgically sectioned when the loaf went through the slicing machine)

◊ A mouse in a bottle of chocolate milk (which actually turned out to be a lump of powdered chocolate flavouring that hadn't dissolved properly)

Source: *A Job Worth Doing: Tales from Health Protection in New Zealand*, edited by Malcom Walker

6 FISHY FOOD FESTIVALS DEDICATED TO KAI MOANA

◊ Whitianga Scallop Festival: a celebration of Whitianga seafood and marine heritage held annually in September. The concept is purist: scallops on a skewer, sizzling off a hot plate, served on a shell … as well as seafood cooking classes and demonstrations.

◊ Bluff Oyster and Food Festival: held annually in May and designed to reflect its motto, 'Unsophisticated and proud of it'. Mid-morning, a pipe band pipes in the oyster and then the feasting begins. Amid competitions for oyster-opening and oyster-eating, visitors can also tuck into crayfish, paua, salmon, blue cod, scallops and whitebait.

◊ Auckland Seafood Festival: the full range of kai moana cooked by celebrity chefs and served up against a backdrop of multitudinous luxury yachts in Auckland's Viaduct Harbour.

◊ Port Chalmers Seafood Festival (biennial): clams, crayfish, green-lipped mussels, whitebait, craft beer and central Otago wine – plus a touch tank of creatures. Run by volunteers to raise money for community groups.

◊ Havelock Mussel and Seafood Festival: mussels prepared more ways than previously thought possible. A mussel-shucking competition is one of the main attractions for the festival that attracts around two thousand visitors annually.

◊ Coromandel Mussel Festival: an all-day serving of many mussel favourites – mussel chowder, fritters, battered mussels, as well as mussels on the half shell and steamed with sauces.

MANDATE FROM THE MINISTRY: 9 TIPS FOR HOLDING A SUCCESSFUL SAUSAGE SIZZLE

The Ministry for Primary Industries tells us how to do better at what we've been doing largely without incident for decades. But if you really want to abide by the rules …

◊ Check with your local council before your event to find out about any requirements they might have.

◊ Organize to collect food as close as possible to the event.

◊ Check that helpers are not ill.

◊ Identify a cash handler who won't touch the food.

◊ Ensure the barbeque operator knows how to cook the sausages safely.

◊ Have equipment available to keep cold food cold.

◊ Have equipment available to store food so it's kept clean and protected from contamination.

◊ Have equipment available to allow for any utensils that could get dirty or soiled (e.g. dropped on the ground) during the event.

· ◊ Have equipment available to clean hands (and replace gloves if used) often during the event.

Source: Ministry for Primary Industries

Chapter
Four

CRIME and CALAMITY:

Dreadful Deeds and Awful Events

DAYS THAT CHANGED NEW ZEALAND

10 July 1985: Sinking of the Rainbow Warrior

Just before midnight, two explosions rip through the hull of the Greenpeace protest ship *Rainbow Warrior,* which has been moored at Marsden Wharf in Auckland. Portuguese-born photographer Fernando Pereira is killed. Within two weeks, two agents of the French secret service, Dominique Prieur and Alain Mafart, will be arrested, charged with murder, and sentenced to 10 years' imprisonment. Outrage against France is fierce, and the repercussions are felt for years. The terrorist action cements in Kiwis a very determined and permanent anti-nuclear stance that is enshrined in Nuclear Free Zone legislation within two years of the bombing.

---

9 CREATIVE CODE NAMES FOR POLICE OPERATIONS

◊ Operation Overdue: the recovery operation in Antarctica following the Erebus disaster.

◊ Operation Stockholm: the operation to find Swedish backpackers Urban Höglin and Heidi Paakkonen.

◊ Operation Satanique: the code name the French foreign intelligence services gave the bombing of the *Rainbow Warrior.*

◊ Operation Tiger: a six-month operation targeting offenders importing into New Zealand Class A and B drugs purchased on the dark net using bitcoin currency.

◊ Operation Fruit: led to the conviction of Wayne Beri, whose criminal activities included drug dealing, trafficking and armed robbery.

◊ Operation Tam: began on 2 January 1998 after the disappearance of Olivia Hope and Ben Smart in the Marlborough Sounds. The code name derives from the charter boat *Tamarack,* which Olivia and her friends had chartered.

◊ Operation Flower: a code name chosen after officers gave the nicknames of Daisy, Tulip and Pansy to three underworld figures manufacturing methamphetamine.

◊ Operation Relentless: involved a zero-tolerance approach to alcohol-related disorder and crime in Auckland City in May 2016.

◊ Operation Ceviche: $300,000 worth of cocaine was seized in a high-profile drug bust in 2016 that netted an award-winning hairdresser, a fashion designer and a member of the Hell's Angels.

LINGERING MYSTERIES: 11 INFAMOUS COLD CASES

◊ **Jennifer Beard,** 31 December 1969. Last seen hitchhiking in the Haast area of the West Coast on New Year's Eve. Her body was discovered 19 days later under the Haast River Bridge.

◊ **Olive Walker,** 15 May 1970. Disappeared on a Friday evening in Rotorua while walking to her sister's house to babysit. Her body was found later that night in a roadside rest area 5 km south of Rotorua.

◊ **Jeanette and Harvey Crewe,** 17 June 1970. Their bodies were discovered in the Waikato River, bound and weighed down. Their 18-month-old daughter, still in her parents' home, was not discovered for five days after their murder. Arthur Allan Thomas was wrongly convicted of the killings.

◊ **Mona Blades,** 31 May 1975. Disappeared while hitchhiking from Hamilton to Hastings. Interest in the case was renewed in 2018 when a documentary claimed initial reports of her being seen getting into an orange Datsun station wagon near Taupo may have been mistaken, and that police hadn't paid enough attention to other apparent sightings. Her body has never been found.

◊ **Tracey Ann Patient,** 29 January 1976. The 13-year-old disappeared while walking home from a friend's house in Auckland. She was strangled, and her body was dumped in the Waitakere Ranges.

◊ **Kirsa Jensen,** 1 September 1983. Rode her horse to the beach at Awatoto, Napier, but didn't return home and has never been seen since. The prime suspect in the case later committed suicide.

◊ **Ernie Abbott,** 27 March 1984. Killed instantly when a booby-trapped suitcase abandoned in the foyer of the Wellington Trades Hall exploded as he tried to remove it. Police suspect he was not the intended target.

◊ **Jane Furlong,** 26 May 1993. The 17-year-old sex worker disappeared from Auckland's Karangahape Road shortly before she was due to give evidence in two criminal trials. Nineteen years later, her skull was discovered buried in Port Waikato sand dunes.

◊ **Claire Hills,** 28 April 1998. A McDonald's crew member on her way to work at Auckland Airport was tied up, placed in the rear of her car and burnt alive. Police thought they had a credible suspect until DNA sampling in 2007 failed to match anyone in their files.

◊ **Kayo Matsuzawa,** 11 September 1998. A 29-year-old Japanese tourist who had checked into a Queen Street hostel in Auckland for three nights was found 10 days later, naked and decomposing, in a fire alarm cupboard in a building near the backpacker's.

◊ **Kirsty Bentley,** 31 December 1998. Murdered while walking her dog along the riverbank in Ashburton. Her body was found near the Rakaia River, nearly 60 km from Ashburton, 17 days later. Suspicion fell on her father and brother, but no one has ever been charged.

Hot wheels:
The 10 most frequently stolen cars

In January 2019, *MoneyHub* magazine published a list of popular cars: those that had been stolen most frequently in the previous six months. The data, gleaned from the NZ Police, showed that choice of hot wheels varied by region. In Auckland City, for example, thieves' primary target was the Mazda Familia; in Wellington, the Mitsubishi Lancer; in Canterbury, the Toyota HiLux.

◊ Toyota HiLux

◊ Subaru Legacy

◊ Subaru Impreza

◊ Holden Commodore

◊ Toyota HiAce

◊ Ford Courier

◊ Honda Accord

◊ Nissan Primera

◊ Toyota Corolla

◊ Mitsubishi Lancer

A captive audience: The most frequently borrowed books from Auckland Prison's libraries

West Library (medium to high security):

◊ *Australian Men's Health* magazine

◊ *Make Me* (Jack Reacher #20), by Lee Child

◊ *3D World* November 2015 magazine

◊ *Wolverine: Weapon X Files,* by Jeff Christiansen

◊ *The Swords of Night and Day,* by David Gemmell

◊ *Life Strategies: The no-nonsense approach to turning your life around,* by Phillip C. McGraw ('Dr Phil')

◊ *Ultimate Spider-Man,* Vol. 19: *Death of a Goblin,* by Brian Bendis

◊ *The Legacy of Captain America,* by Joe Simon

◊ *Undisputed Truth: My autobiography,* by Mike Tyson

East Library (maximum security wing):

◊ *Carte Blanche* by Jeffery Deaver

◊ *100 Facts on Ancient Egypt* by Jane Walker

◊ *100 Facts on Oceans* by Clare Oliver

◊ *100 Greatest Wonders of the World* by Mark Truman

◊ *100 Myths about the Middle East* by Fred Halliday

◊ *100 Things* by Sebastian Terry

◊ *10,000 Dreams Interpreted: A dictionary of dreams,* by Gustavus Hindman Miller

- ◊ *1001 Facts about Wild Animals,* by Moira Butterfield

- ◊ *1001 Muscle Car Facts,* by Steve Magnante

- ◊ *The 1001 Wonders of the Universe* by Piers Bizony

INJUSTICE FOR ALL: 7 CASES OF WRONGFUL CONVICTION

- ◊ Teina Pora: wrongly convicted of the rape and murder of Auckland woman Susan Burdett in 1992. Spent 21 years in prison.

- ◊ Arthur Allan Thomas: wrongly convicted of the murders of Jeanette and Harvey Crewe in 1970. Spent 9 years in prison.

- ◊ David Bain: wrongly convicted of the murder of his parents, two sisters and one brother in 1994. Spent 13 years in prison.

- ◊ David Dougherty: wrongly convicted of the abduction and rape of an 11-year-old Auckland schoolgirl. Spent 3 years in prison.

- ◊ Lucy Akatere, McCushla Fuataha and Tania Vini: three teenagers wrongfully convicted of the aggravated robbery of a 16-year-old schoolgirl in 1999. Spent 7 months in prison.

- ◊ Aaron Farmer: wrongly convicted of raping a 22-year-old woman in Christchurch in 2003. Spent 2 years in prison.

- ◊ Phillip Johnston and Jaden Knight: wrongly convicted of a late-night arson at Foxton's Manawatu Hotel in 2004. Spent 9 months in prison.

FOR THE RECORD: 4 LAWYERS WHO'VE WRITTEN BOOKS

◊ Christopher Harder: *Mercy, Mistress, Mercy* (a recount from the defence lawyer in the prosecution of Neville Walker and Renee Chignell for the murder of cricket umpire Peter Plumley Walker).

◊ Peter Williams: *The Dwarf Who Moved* (about people such as Arthur Allen Thomas and 'Mr Asia', and the cases that defined his high-profile career as a criminal barrister).

◊ Colin Amery: *Always the Outsider: A lawyer's journey* (a memoir from the prosecution lawyer in the Rainbow Warrior bombers' trial, covering his travels, adventures, and eventual return to the law at the age of 50).

◊ L P Leary: *Not Entirely Legal* (the autobiography of the celebrated advocate who would arrive at the court in striped trousers, spats and homburg, but by afternoon be in his orchard, dressed in a pair of old army trousers cut off at the knee).

6 things New Zealand could expect
if all drugs were decriminalized

Portugal decriminalized the personal possession of all drugs in 2001. People dependent on drugs are now encouraged to seek treatment but are rarely sanctioned if they choose not to. The move to decriminalize was prompted by soaring numbers of drug-related deaths and rapidly increasing rates of HIV, AIDS, tuberculosis, and hepatitis B and C among people who injected drugs. Although statistics on drug use are keenly disputed, clear patterns have emerged.

By following the Portuguese example, New Zealand could expect:

◊ A decrease in the rate of drug use among all adults aged 15 to 64

◊ A decline in the prevalence of drug-related infectious diseases

◊ A reduction in the number of people arrested and sent to court for drug offences

◊ A reduction in the incidence of drug-related crime, such as thefts from homes and businesses

◊ A decline in the proportion of drug-related offenders in the prison population

◊ An increased need for programmes that prevent and reduce the harm of drug use, together with improved social reintegration programmes for drug users.

Detectives' notebook:
9 infamous addresses and the names they invoke

◊ 115 Bassett Road, Remuera, Auckland (John Gillies and Ronald Jorgensen)

◊ 65 Every St, Andersons Bay, Dunedin (David Bain)

◊ 30 Karamea Crescent, Palmerston North (Mark Lundy)

◊ 43 Judds Rd, Masterton, now a park (Raymond Ratima)

◊ 27 Muri Street, Aramoana (David Gray)

◊ 26A Rotomahana Crescent, Remuera, Auckland (Peter Plumley Walker and Renee Chignell)

◊ 49 Okiato Road, Russell (built for Terry Clark, 'Mr Asia')

◊ 101 Deans Ave and 223A Linwood Ave, Christchurch (a gunman we choose not to name)

---

15 DISASTERS THAT BROKE KIWI HEARTS

◊ 7 February 1863: shipwreck of HMS *Orpheus,* Manukau Harbour. Death toll: 189

◊ 10 June 1886: eruption of Mt Tarawera. Death toll: 120

◊ 26 March 1896: Brunner mine explosion. Death toll: 65

◊ 3 February 1931: Napier earthquake, measuring 7.8 on the Richter scale. Death toll: 256

◊ 18 November 1947: fire at Ballantyne's Department Store, Christchurch. Death toll: 41

◊ 24 December 1953: Tangiwai rail disaster. Death toll: 151

◊ 3 July 1963: DC-3 airliner crash in the Kaimai Range, Bay of Plenty. Death toll: 23

◊ 19 January 1967: explosion in the Strongman mine, near Greymouth. Death toll: 19

◊ 9 April 1968: sinking of the *Wahine* at the entrance to Wellington Harbour. Death toll: 51

◊ 28 November 1979: crash of an Air New Zealand DC-10 airliner into Mt Erebus, Antarctica. Death toll: 257

◊ 7 March 1988: Cyclone Bola, East Coast. Death toll: 4

◊ 28 April 1995: collapse of a viewing platform at Cave Creek on the West Coast. Death toll: 14

◊ 19 and 24 November 2010: Pike River mine explosion. Death toll: 29

◊ 22 February 2011, Christchurch earthquake. Death toll: 185

◊ 14 November 2016: Kaikōura earthquake. Death toll: 2

CLICK 'N' FIX: 9 CAUSES THAT SPURRED KIWIS TO HASHTAG ACTIVISM

Feel bad about something? Show your concern by clicking your mouse ... sign a petition, 'like' a page, post a comment, retweet a few words. It will really make a difference, apparently. You are a social justice warrior – unless you absorb an advertising message created for Crisis Relief Singapore (CRS). The campaign featured images of people struggling or in need, surrounded by many people giving a thumbs-up. The caption pointed out that 'Liking isn't helping'.

Hashtag activism Kiwis 'liked' on Facebook:

◊ #MeToo. Meant to make people aware of how many women have been sexually harassed or assaulted. Spread virally in the wake of sexual misconduct allegations against Harvey Weinstein.

◊ #JeSuisCharlie. Adopted by supporters of freedom of speech and freedom of the press after the 7 January 2015 shooting in which 12 people were killed at the offices of the French satirical weekly newspaper *Charlie Hebdo*.

◊ #BlackLivesMatter. An international movement to campaign against violence and systemic racism towards black people.

◊ #IStandWithAhmed. A declaration of solidarity with the teen who was arrested after bringing to his school in Texas a homemade clock that administrators believed looked like a bomb.

◊ #BooksNotBullets. Launched by Malala Yousafzai with the hope that world leaders would consider redirecting eight days' worth of military spending for educational pursuits. According to the Malala Fund Blog, this act would raise $39 billion which could 'provide 12 years of free, quality education to every child on the planet'.

◊ #LoveIsLove. The LGBT community is just like everybody else, so who cares who you love?

◊ #RedPeak. Resulted in a fifth design being added to the referendum measuring Kiwis' support for an alternative design for the New Zealand flag.

◊ #BringBackGeorgiePie. Nostalgia gripped lovers of McDonald's Georgie Pie until the company relented and the classic mince steak and cheese pie was reinstated on its menu.

◊ #PinkPussyHat. Launched in solidarity with women's marches in the United States in protest at Donald Trump's 'grab them by the pussy' remarks. The pattern for the hat was shared by hundreds of thousands of women around the globe.

STAYING SAFE: 17 ITEMS CONSUMER NZ WANTS TO SEE IN YOUR EMERGENCY SURVIVAL KIT

◊ A backpack

◊ A metal torch

◊ AA/AAA alkaline batteries 4-pack

◊ A pocket radio

◊ Face masks to filter dust and fumes

◊ Hand sanitizer

◊ Anti-bacterial wet wipes

◊ Pocket tissues

◊ A drink bottle

◊ Work gloves

◊ A Pocket Survival bag from the New Zealand Mountain Safety Council

◊ An emergency poncho

◊ Water purification tablets

◊ Three days' worth of emergency food rations

◊ First aid kit

◊ Duct tape

◊ Rubbish bags

Source: Consumer NZ

5 MASSIVE FALSEHOODS QUASHED
BY THE WEBSITE SNOPES

Snopes is an online fact-checking website with a reputation for impartiality in debunking or confirming urban legends. In mid-2017, it was receiving around 20 million visitors per month. Around 80 per cent of these visits originated in the United States, but Kiwi content still manages to make an appearance.

HOAX There is a volcano in NZ from which fuchsia-coloured smoke billows.

FACT The 'pink volcano' video was created by artist Filip Hodas and shared to his Facebook page in December 2016. The only volcanos that emit bright pink smoke are those created by digital artists.

HOAX A 26-year-old tourist from New Zealand died in Pensacola, Florida, while trying to take a selfie with an alligator.

FACT The article *did* appear in April 2017 on what appeared to be a regional news outlet, the *Florida Sun Post*. However, the site, which purports to be the digital version of a local newspaper, is fake.

HOAX Ruth Bader Ginsburg, Justice of the US Supreme Court, resigned her seat and moved to New Zealand.

FACT During an interview with the *New York Times* in July 2016, Ginsburg said that if Donald Trump became president it would be 'time to move to New Zealand'. Her jokey comment was quickly embellished into a declaration that Ginsburg has resigned, retired and relocated. On 23 February 2017, however, more than two weeks after her supposed translocation, she appeared on BBC television, and no mention was made of any intention to observe America's future from the safe distance of Aotearoa.

HOAX A video shows a 15.5 metre-long giant squid washed up on a beach in Punakaiki on the West Coast, on 1 March 2015.

FACT The image has been digitally altered. The original image was taken when a humpback whale beached itself in White Rock, British Columbia, Canada, in June 2012. The giant-squid-in-Punakaiki image was created by cropping the original image and replacing the whale with a photograph of a squid.

HOAX On 27 October 2014, an outline of a giant cat appeared in Auckland on Google Maps, in the form of a remote pathway.

FACT By the time it was reported (and had garnered a sizeable response), Google had already discovered and removed the fake image, saying it would investigate the 'anomaly'.

WHY SO SAD: 6 OFFICIAL ATTEMPTS TO PATCH THINGS UP

Official apologies have spiked in the past three decades, but they are nothing new. In 1077, Henry IV, the Holy Roman Emperor, trekked over the Alps and then knelt in the snow for three days to apologize to Pope Gregory VII for usurping papal authority and appointing his own bishops. He begged to be taken back into the Roman Catholic Church from which the Pope had excommunicated him.

A more recent public apology was made in 2007 by the Danish minister of culture, who apologized to the Irish for Viking raids that had taken place over 1200 years previously. (Presumably, he enjoyed his own joke.)

Nevertheless, when a government apologizes to its own citizens or those of another country, the expressions of regret and remorse are preserved as part of the historical record, even if nobody has knelt in the snow to make them.

Significant apologies from the New Zealand government include those made to:

◊ The descendants of the community of Parihaka for the colonial forces' treatment of the community during the Crown's attempt to confiscate land on 5 November 1881. On that day, the troops were greeted by children who sang and offered loaves of bread. Parihaka's leaders were arrested and held without trial for 16 months. The apology was delivered by Attorney-General Chris Finlayson, who said, 'The sense of grievance that arises from that history is anything but historical. It's remembered; it's lived every day. That is why the Crown comes today offering an apology to the people of Parihaka for actions that were committed in its name almost 140 years ago'.

◊ Vietnam veterans, for the failure of successive governments to address their concerns, including exposure to Agent Orange and other toxic defoliants. Prime Minister Helen Clark delivered the apology in a ministerial statement to parliament on 28 May 2008, and said, 'The Crown extends to New Zealand Vietnam Veterans and their families an apology for the manner in which their loyal service in the name of New Zealand was not recognized as it should have been, when it should have been, and for inadequate support extended to them and their families after their return home from the conflict'.

◊ The Chinese community, for the imposition of a poll tax from 1881 until 1944. Chinese entering New Zealand were legally required to pay a tax of ten pounds initially, and one hundred pounds eventually – although no other ethnic group was subjected to such restrictions or tax. Chinese were also denied the right to naturalisation for more than 40 years. The apology was delivered during Chinese New Year celebrations at Parliament in 2002 by Prime Minister Helen Clark, who said the government wished to formally apologize 'to those Chinese people who paid the poll tax and suffered other discrimination imposed by statute and to their descendants … we also express our sorrow and regret that such practices were once considered appropriate.'

◊ The people of Samoa for 'the injustices arising from New Zealand's administration of Samoa in its earlier years'. The apology, delivered by Prime Minister Helen Clark in 2002 at a state luncheon in Apia marking the fortieth anniversary of Samoan independence, referred to the decision by New Zealand authorities to allow a ship carrying passengers with influenza to dock in Apia in 1918, which caused one of the world's worst recorded epidemics, killing more than one-fifth of Samoa's population.

◊ Homosexuals whose criminal convictions for historical homosexual offenses remained on record, even after 1986, when consensual sex between men aged 16 and over was decriminalized. Before the Criminal Records (Expungement of Convictions for Historical Homosexual Offences) Bill was passed into law, the convictions could appear in criminal history checks. Delivering the apology in Parliament on 6 July 2017, MP Amy Adams noted: 'Today we are putting on the record that this house deeply regrets the hurt and stigma suffered by the many hundreds of New Zealand men who were turned into criminals by a law that was profoundly wrong, and for that, we are sorry'.

◊ At her post-Cabinet press conference on 10 December 2018, Prime Minister Jacinda Ardern addressed the family of a murdered tourist, 22-year-old Grace Millane. 'From the Kiwis I have spoken to, there is this overwhelming sense of hurt and shame that this has happened in our country, a place that prides itself on our hospitality, on our manaakitanga, especially to those who are visiting our shores. So on behalf of New Zealand, I want to apologize to Grace's family.' With an audible catch in her voice, she added, 'Your daughter should have been safe here, and she wasn't, and I'm sorry for that'.

...and one apology we could have done without

'I'm sorry for being a man.' – David Cunliffe's unusual apology at a Women's Refuge forum on 4 July 2014, while launching Labour's domestic violence policy.

Chapter
Five

BUSINESS and MONEY:
Wheeling and Dealing

Days that changed New Zealand

20 October 1987: The stock market crash of 1987

A gambling mentality – the conviction that there are ways to make a lot of money quite easily – has led many to invest in companies like Chase Corporation and Equiticorp without adequate research or historical perspective. The deregulated market has been performing feverishly – until now. Following a dramatic drop on Wall Street, the New Zealand stock market plunges 15 per cent in one day. The euphoria evaporates as mum-and-dad investors are dragged under, businesses go bust, and the country learns that wealth is sometimes illusory. The next generation of investors turn away from capital markets and focus on property instead.

Creative genius: 12 infuriatingly memorable advertising slogans

◊ Spray and walk away (30 Seconds)

◊ World famous in New Zealand since ages ago (Lemon & Paeroa)

◊ The world's warmest welcome (Air New Zealand)

◊ You just can't beat the Mad Butcher's meat (The Mad Butcher)

◊ DIY? It's in our DNA (Mitre 10)

- ◊ It's finest cheddar, made better (Chesdale cheese)

- ◊ Where everyone gets a bargain (The Warehouse)

- ◊ You'll never buy better (Briscoes)

- ◊ No one's got more sports gear (Rebel Sports)

- ◊ Pride of the South (Speight's)

- ◊ Our policy is New Zealand's lowest food prices (PAK'nSAVE)

- ◊ Remember: It works, you don't (Wet & Forget)

---

8 USES FOR THE 10-CENT COIN IF IT BECOMES OBSOLETE

Hand it back! The Reserve Bank pays face value for currency that has been legally issued for use in New Zealand but has ceased to be legal tender (including pre-decimal currency).

- ◊ A coin can be used to steady a wobbly computer stand or even a table leg.

- ◊ Giving anyone an empty wallet as a gift brings bad luck. Slip the coin in to neutralize the curse.

- ◊ If you're building a new boat in a traditional style, slip a coin underneath the mast before it is raised. This ancient Roman tradition is still practised today because it is thought to bring good fortune.

- ◊ The well-known tradition of the bride wearing 'something old, something new' originally stems from the rhyme, 'Something old, something new, something borrowed, something blue, and a silver sixpence in her shoe.' A silver sixpence in the bride's shoe is a traditional good luck wedding gesture and, customarily, it is the father of the bride who places the sixpence as a symbol of his wish for prosperity, love and love and happiness in her marriage. Kiwi brides will have to make do with a 10-cent piece.

◊ If you wear garters to keep your knee socks up, keep a coin handy in case of garter breakage. If the garter gives way, simply pull the coin and sock through the metal hanger and sartorial standards will not be comprized.

◊ Place one on a railway track and check the effect of a train passing over it.

◊ Contribute them to charity coin collections.

MONEY-MAKERS: THE EYE-WATERING WEALTH OF 12 KIWI BILLIONAIRES AND HOW THEY DID IT

Graeme Hart	Packaging, investment	$10 billion
Peter Thiel	Technology, investment	$4 billion
Todd family	Energy, investment	$4 billion
Richard Chandler	Energy, banking, healthcare	$3 billion
Mowbray family	Toy manufacturing	$3 billion
Goodman family	Property investment, development	$2.4 billion
Sir Michael Friedlander	Property, investment	$1.85 billion
Erceg family	Liquor, horticulture	$1.8 billion
Christopher Chandler	Investment, philanthropy	$1.5 billion
Soichiro Fukutake	Education, art, investment	$1.4 billion

| Stephen Jennings | Investment banking | $1.1 billion |
| Pye family | Agriculture ventures | $1 billion |

10 EXPRESSIONS BELOVED BY THE REAL ESTATE INDUSTRY AND WHAT THEY REALLY MEAN

◊ Grand old lady – It's run-down and in a desperate state.

◊ Secluded row – It's so far down a narrow track it's lying at the bottom of a scrub-covered gully.

◊ Land with potential – The section is too steep to sensibly build on (Wellington is an exception) or the ground is unstable and covered with rubbish.

◊ Refreshed and ready – It's had a quick tart-up with a paintbrush and a superficial tidy. Don't look too closely – and certainly not in the cupboards.

◊ A strong sense of community – Everyone knows everyone else's business and they like to keep it that way.

◊ Character cottage – The layout is unusual and probably dysfunctional, and the whole house undoubtedly needs renovation. DIYers have had a go, but their workmanship leaves a lot to be desired.

◊ Fabulous during the summer months – Those holes in the wall and the loo that's collapsed through the floor will allow the air to circulate.

◊ It's got a great 'cosy factor' – It's so small that it's cheap to heat.

◊ Double glazing and a tall hedge protect you from outside noise – The house is only 10 metres from the motorway, and the windows rattle every time a truck roars past.

◊ Such a good buy for creative people – It's a do-up.

12 KIWI COLLECTIBLES THAT PROVE DE-CLUTTERING IS A WASTE OF MONEY

De-cluttering is good for peace of mind, because it creates space – both mental and physical. But it also robs you of the joy that comes with discovering that some tatty old bit of rubbish you've been storing in the back of the garage for 20 years is now worth some serious money.

An Auckland antiques dealer lists a few bits and pieces that have taken breathtaking leaps in value over the last two decades:

	1999	2019
◊ *Edmond's Cookbook,* 1962 edition	$15	$43
◊ Feltex pictorial rug of the Auckland Harbour Bridge	$50	$800
◊ 1 kg of clear kauri gum	$25	$1000
◊ Green McAlpine Crown Lynn jug	$45	$285
◊ Large Crown Lynn swan	$29	$345
◊ Ernest Shufflebotham large ribbed vase by Crown Lynn	$300	$865
◊ Wharetana bookends	$800	$4000
◊ Cup and saucer from an Air New Zealand dinner set	$35	$250
◊ Big Tree petrol enamel sign	$475	$3000
◊ Silver Fern tobacco tin	$15	$40
◊ Large Fun Ho truck	$45	$225
◊ Auckland bus blind	$0	$450

Source: Malcolm Grover, Country Antiques, Auckland

6 Kiwi models whose face is their fortune

◊ Ashleigh Good: 1.82 m tall, with dark brown hair and blue eyes. She made headlines when she strutted down the Chanel runway, seven months pregnant, hand-in-hand with Karl Lagerfeld. She was also on the cover of Italian *Vogue* in November 2013.

◊ Georgia Fowler: 1.77 m tall, with light brown hair and blue/green eyes. She appeared in Victoria's Secret's annual fashion show in 2016 and a Selena Gomez music video ('It Ain't Me') in 2017.

◊ Holly Rose Emery: 1.80 m tall, with blonde hair and blue eyes. In 2013, she appeared on the cover of Australian *Vogue,* for which she did the photoshoot on her seventeenth birthday, as well as runway shows for Prada, Dolce & Gabbana, Marc Jacobs and Miu Miu. Also known for a medically supervised weight loss of 36 kg before becoming a model.

◊ Kylie Bax: 1.78 m tall, with blonde hair and grey/green eyes. Featured in *Sports Illustrated's* Swimsuit Issue in 2000, as well as on numerous international magazine covers, including more than 20 *Vogue* covers around the world. She has strutted the catwalks for designers such as Chanel, Christian Dior, and Alexander McQueen.

◊ Rachel Hunter: 1.80 m tall, with blonde hair and blue eyes. Has been visible almost everywhere, starting from when she was the 'Trumpet girl' for Tip Top ice creams and most recently as the star of her own TV series, *Tour of Beauty*. She featured on the cover of *Sports Illustrated's* Swimsuit Issue in 1994 and again in 2006.

◊ Stella Maxwell: 1.75 m tall, with blonde hair and blue eyes. Modelled at the Victoria's Secret fashion show 2014, and in high-profile ad campaigns for ASOS, Alexander McQueen, H&M and Urban Outfitters. Has also appeared in *Vogue* and *Elle* magazines.

WINSTON'S MULTI-PURPOSE PRESENT: 13 HANDY USES FOR A SUPERGOLD CARD

The SuperGold Card does so much more than get you over to Waiheke Island for free. At a pinch, this rigid yet flexible bit of laminate can substitute for a range of tools. Use your SuperGold Card to:

◊ Remove chewing gum from the soles of your shoes

◊ Scrape ice off your windscreen

◊ Mark your place in the book you're reading

◊ Slice cheesecake or pizza

◊ Mask sections you don't want painted when working in a tight space

◊ Ease open a doorknob or spring latch (but no good on a dead bolt, alas)

◊ Rule a nice straight (short) line

◊ Extract old grout from between thinly spaced tiles

◊ Give a smooth, convex finish to new grout around sinks, baths and shower enclosures

◊ Play the guitar if you've lost your pick

◊ Scrape out weeds from between paving stones

◊ Substitute as a splint for your broken finger until you get to A&E

◊ Practise your golf putting by attaching it to a pole and swinging.

The price we paid for beauty:
10 products in Farmers' 1935
mail order catalogue

Remember shillings and pence? Converted to their decimal equivalents – allowing for inflation, even – some prices seem surprising today.

◊ A bottle of Yardley's Old English Lavender perfume No. 1671   2/6

◊ A tin of Morny's June Roses talcum powder   2/9

◊ A box of Cashmere Bouquet face powder   1/3

◊ A packet of Butywave shampoo powder   6d

◊ A cake of Wright's Coal Tar Toilet Soap   9d

◊ A tube of Palmolive shaving cream   1/6

◊ A tube of Ipana toothpaste   1/3

◊ Beetham's Glycerine and Cucumber hair preparation   2/-

◊ A bottle of Odor-o-no deodorant   2/9

◊ A tin of Carnation Corn Caps   1/3

7 THINGS FIVE-STAR HOTELS DON'T WANT YOU TO DO IN YOUR ROOM

Hotels are required to turn a blind eye to many things, and some, like the Chelsea Hotel in New York, build their legend around the unruly celebrity guests who've stayed. Generally, though, bad behaviour is not condoned, and it isn't good for business. If only guests would obey certain rules, hospitality would be easier to offer.

◊ Don't use the iron to toast bread and don't cook spaghetti or two-minute noodles in the electric jug. Definitely do not boil your knickers. Tea never quite tastes the same.

◊ Don't do anything that sets off the fire alarm. At least four fire trucks will attend at a cost to the hotel of $1500 per fire truck. In the case of high rises, six fire trucks will show up.

◊ Don't make so much noise that other guests complain. Rowdiness is usually unleashed by drunkenness, and both are ugly and tedious to deal with.

◊ Don't tamper with the bottles in the minibar. Don't puncture fizzy-drink cans from the underneath to drain the contents or refill partly consumed bottles with water or tea. Watered-down spirits are irritating for the guests who discover the problem and embarrassing for the hotel.

◊ Don't stand on the toilet seat to use the facility. It leaves footprints and compromises hygiene. Take a seat, please.

◊ Don't leave half your luggage behind when you go. Guests with plans to become overstayers often do so by exiting through the lobby with a minimum of belongings in order not to draw attention to themselves. They then melt invisibly into the local population and have long gone by the time their absence is noted and the hotel management is required to call in the police.

◊ Don't die. It's very upsetting for housekeeping to discover you in such a state.

Source: John Farrell, Senior Consultant, Horwath HTL, New Zealand

PAYING UP: THE 7 LARGEST TREATY OF WAITANGI CLAIMS AND SETTLEMENTS

1992	Fisheries (the 'Sealord' deal)	$170 million
1995	Waikato–Tainui Raupatu	$170 million
1997	Ngai Tahu	$170 million
2008	Central North Island Forests Iwi Collective (the 'Treelords' deal)	$161 million
2008	Taranaki Whanui ki Te Upoko o Te Ika	$45.1 million
2003	Ngati Awa	$43.3 million
2008	Te Arawa Affiliate Iwi and Hapu	$38.6 million

THE ENTERTAINMENT BUDGET: 4 RED CARPET OCCASIONS

◊ Cost of the Royal Visit of William and Kate, together with baby George, to New Zealand in 2014: $1,035,000

◊ Cost of the Royal Visit of Charles and Camilla to New Zealand in 2015: $1,395,876

◊ Cost of the Royal Visit of Harry to New Zealand in 2015: $426,317

◊ Cost of the Royal Visit of Harry and Meghan to New Zealand in 2018: $1,007,729

WHAT GLASS CEILING?
6 KIWI WOMEN WHO'VE BROKEN THROUGH

◊ Farah Palmer. First woman elected to the board of New Zealand Rugby, and Chair of the NZ Maori Rugby Board.

◊ Linda Jenkinson. Serial entrepreneur and multimillionaire businesswoman, who, in 1998, became the second Kiwi ever to float a company on the Nasdaq stock exchange in the United States. Her current appointments include director at Air New Zealand.

◊ Cecilia Robinson. Created food kit delivery business My Food Bag in 2013 with her husband, James Robinson, together with chef Nadia Lim and businesswoman Theresa Gattung. The company now has more than 50,000 customers.

◊ Wendy Pye. Her publishing company, Sunshine Books, publishes early learning material for literacy and maths and is considered one of the world's most successful educational export companies. Pye is now one of New Zealand's richest women.

◊ Mavis Mullins. Under her management, her family's shearing business became the first in the world to achieve ISO 9002 accreditation. In 2000, Mullins headed the launch of the mobile network 2degrees, which has helped create a more competitive environment for telcos.

◊ Suzie Moncrieff. Transformed the World of Wearable Art from a novelty event for Nelson designers to a global phenomenon that brings together more than 300 designers and a crew of over 400 for a week of sold-out performances in Wellington each year.

NICE LITTLE EARNERS:
15 SALARIES YOU MIGHT SELL YOUR SOUL FOR

The remuneration packages of some chief executives (information accurate at June 2018):

◊	Governor of the Reserve Bank	Mr Adrian Orr $1,217,000
◊	Accident Compensation Corporation	Mr Scott Pickering $830,000 to $839,999
◊	University of Auckland	Prof. Stuart McCutcheon $760,000 to $769,999
◊	Commissioner of Police	Mr Mike Bush $700,000 to $709,999
◊	Inland Revenue Department	Ms Naomi Ferguson $670,000 to $679,999
◊	Chief of the NZ Defence Force	Lt Gen. Tim Keating $670,000 to $679,999
◊	Department of Internal Affairs	Mr Colin MacDonald $660,000 to $669,999
◊	Solicitor-General	Ms Una Jagose $660,000 to $669,999
◊	Housing New Zealand Corporation	Mr Andrew McKenzie

	$640,000 to $649,999
◊ The Treasury	Mr Gabriel Makhlouf $640,000 to $649,999
◊ New Zealand Transport Agency	Mr Fergus Gammie $640,000 to $649,999
◊ New Zealand Trade and Enterprise	Mr Peter Chrisp $630,000 to $639,999
◊ State Services Commissioner	Mr Peter Hughes $620,000 to $629,999
◊ Financial Markets Authority	Mr Rob Everett $610,000 to $619,999
◊ Department of the Prime Minister	Mr Andrew Kibblewhite $610,000 to $619,999

But wait, there's more!
What 10 New Zealand CEOs earned in FY 17

◊ Theo Spierings (Fonterra)	$8.3 million
◊ Christopher Luxon (Air New Zealand)	$4.6 million
◊ David Hisco (ANZ Banking)	$3.7 million
◊ Adrian Littlewood (Auckland Intl. Airport)	$3.3 million
◊ Simon Moulter (Spark)	$2.69 million

◊ Russel Creedy (Restaurant Brands)	$2.44 million
◊ Mark Binns (Meridian Energy)	$2.37 million
◊ David McLean (Westpac NZ)	$2.29 million
◊ Mike Bennetts (Z Energy)	$2.27 million
◊ Mark Adamson (Fletcher Building)	$2.09 million

7 Kiwi companies that foreign buyers paid big bikkies for

◊ TradeMe (online auctions): bought by British private equity firm Apax Partners in 2019 for $2.56 billion.

◊ Sistema (plastic kitchen containers): bought by Newell Brands in 2016 for $660 million.

◊ Wildfire (social media marketing): bought by Google in 2012 for $487 million.

◊ Tip Top (ice cream): bought by global dairy giant Froneri in 2019 for $380 million.

◊ Ezibuy (clothing): bought by Woolworths in 2013 for $350 million.

◊ 42 Below (vodka): bought by Bacardi in 2006 for $138 million.

◊ Charlie's (juices): bought by Asahi in 2011 for $129 million.

8 REASONS FEMALE TRADIES ARE IN DEMAND BY KIWI BUILDING COMPANIES

It doesn't take brute strength to bang a nail into a piece of wood, so there's no reason to stick with any old-fashioned notions about building being blokes' business. These days, the call for women to learn a trade keeps getting louder – and for some very good reasons.

◊ Clients feel safer alone in the house with them

◊ They're better able to multi-task

◊ They're more likely to turn up on time

◊ They're better communicators

◊ They pay more attention to detail

◊ They obey safety instructions without objecting

◊ They are not under the illusion that they are indestructible, so they work more safely

◊ They don't thrash equipment and vehicles the way male tradies do.

OVERSEAS INVESTMENTS: 7 COUNTRIES WITH BANKS IN NEW ZEALAND

◊ Australia (ANZ, BNZ, ASB, Westpac, Commonwealth Bank)

◊ China (HSBC, Bank of China, China Construction Bank, Industrial and Commercial Bank of China)

◊ India (Bank of Baroda, Bank of India)

- ◊ Japan (Bank of Tokyo-Mitsubishi)
- ◊ Korea (Kookmin Bank)
- ◊ The Netherlands (Rabobank)
- ◊ United States (Citibank, JP Morgan Chase Bank)

---

13 PERSONALIZED PLATES WITH HEFTY PRICE TAGS

Marketplaces for personalized plates are many, and while some sellers humbly request merely that a sensible offer be made, other sellers dream big. In March 2018, ambitious listings from websites like MrPlates, Numberplates and TradeMe included:

◊	1NHIM	$71,000
◊	IM R1CH	$50,000
◊	LØYAL	$50,000
◊	MAORI	$49,000
◊	8EGHT8	$48,000
◊	KEY4PM	$30,000
◊	T8 A T8	$25,000
◊	GØDSGD	$25,000
◊	DRUMS	$20,000
◊	FRODO	$15,000
◊	HØ1D3N	$13,500
◊	L8TAM8	$10,000
◊	GØLLUM	$10,000

…and 7 more pedestrian options

◊	SAYTAN	$7666
◊	2FUGLY	$5000
◊	33333V	$3333
◊	ØE 666 (Naughty Devil)	$2500
◊	CØWPØØ	$1500
◊	MY ØFIS	$1500
◊	STAFKA	$1200

THE 8 BEST KIWI SHOP NAMES

◊ Merchant of Venison: Christchurch-based seller of South Island venison to butchers, supermarkets, restaurants and the general public throughout New Zealand

◊ Starchi & Starchi: a drycleaner's in the Highland Park shopping centre, Auckland

◊ Tequila Mockingbird: until February 2017, a tapas restaurant in Christchurch

◊ Piston Cranky Motors: an auto services specialist in Christchurch

◊ Alley Barbers: a hairdresser's in Porirua

◊ The Carpenter's Daughter: plus-size fashion outlet in Auckland

◊ The Stray Possum Lodge: accommodation on Great Barrier Island

◊ Khyber Spice Invader: Auckland suppliers of Indian spices and grocery items.

...and 9 overseas businesses we'd love to see in the malls

◊ Bread Pitt (a food outlet in Singapore)

◊ Back to the Fuchsia (florists in the UK)

◊ Frying Nemo (a fish and chip shop in Australia)

◊ World of Woolcraft (a wool shop in the UK)

◊ Iron Maiden (an ironing service in the UK)

◊ Sew It Seams (a clothing alteration service in Canada)

◊ Spex in the City (an optometrist's in the UK)

◊ Cash 22 (a pawnbroker in the UK)

◊ Spruce Springclean (window and gutter cleaners in the UK).

Chapter

Six

SCIENCE and NATURE:

The Great Outdoors

DAYS THAT CHANGED NEW ZEALAND

22 February 2011: The Christchurch earthquake

At 12.51 pm, a magnitude 6.3 earthquake strikes at a shallow depth 10 km southeast of Christchurch's central business district, causing severe damage in Christchurch and Lyttelton. The violent shaking causes the CTV building to collapse, killing 130 people. Falling masonry kills 11 others, and eight die when two city buses are crushed under collapsing walls. Several thousand are injured. Liquefaction seeps through properties and over streets, and many thousands of homes are found to be damaged beyond repair. New Zealand's first national state of emergency is declared on 23 February. The repair bill will exceed $45 billion.

NEW ZEALAND'S WEATHER IN PLAIN ENGLISH:
7 INFORMATIVE QUOTES

◊ 'We have a great deal of disagreeable weather, and a small proportion of bad weather, but in no other part of the world, I believe, does Nature so thoroughly understand how to make a fine day as in New Zealand.' – Lady Mary Anne Barker in *Station Life in New Zealand* (published 1870)

◊ 'I tell you what is, this country wants roofing-in badly. I am going back to Australia.' – Alexander Bathgate, *Waiatarua*, 1881

◊ 'All of New Zealand's winds are interesting. Some, like the dry northwesterly of the Canterbury Plains in summer, is reputed to drive farmers' wives mad, although why it should be sexually selective in this way is not clear.' – Keith Ovenden, *Ratatui*, 1984

◊ 'It's so dry here the trees are running after the dogs.' – Central Otago farmer, TV One News, 3 March 1999.

◊ 'The rain is a goneburger but the showers and a bit of frost, well, they're sort of come burgers, if you know what I mean.' – Jim Hickey, TV One weatherman, 2002

◊ 'Pretty nasty spell of weather coming our way ... You'd almost think that Mother Nature has, *phttt*, spit the dummy – and in a big way.' – Dan Corbett, TVNZ weatherman, 2017

◊ 'If you can't see Mt Egmont, it's raining. If you can, it's going to rain.' – Local saying

------

THE NATION'S PETS:
9 ANIMALS KIWIS HAVE LOVED

◊ Paddles the Cat: a ginger and white polydactyl cat, owned by Jacinda Ardern. Paddles interrupted a congratulatory phone call from US President Donald Trump by entering the newly elected prime minister's lounge and meowing loudly. Despite a huge social media presence, Paddles' fame was short-lived. He was hit by a car and killed on 7 November 2017.

◊ Nigel 'No Mates': a gannet dubbed 'the loneliest bird in the world' which lived on Mana Island, off the Porirua coast, amid a colony of nearly 80 concrete birds conservationists had installed to encourage other gannets to join him. Nigel must have had a very good imagination (or a very small bird brain), because he loved his fake friends, and for four years he tried valiantly to woo one of them by constructing a nest of seaweed, mud and twigs. News of his sudden death at the end of January 2018, just as three real birds had joined the colony, reverberated around the world. Lovelorn Nigel's lifeless body was found in the nest that he had made for his cold-hearted concrete 'partner'.

◊ Charisma: the horse that equestrian Mark Todd rode to Olympic triumph. The nation loved Charisma's dainty cross-steps in dressage events. It was a jaunty move not many would have predicted achievable by the horse also known as 'Podge', possibly as a consequence of his habit of eating his own bedding.

◊ Opo the Gay Dolphin: a bottlenose dolphin that delighted beach-goers at Hokianga Harbour in the 1950s. She would allow children to swim beside her or even ride on her back.

◊ Henry the Tuatara: Henry had been eschewing sex for decades when, in 2008, he was caught fornicating with Mildred, aged somewhere in her seventies. Around seven months later, Mildred laid 12 eggs, 11 of which hatched successfully, making Henry a father at 111 years of age.

◊ Old Blue: a black robin in the Chatham Islands that, in 1976, was the last remaining fertile female of her species. With the delicate and discreet assistance of a conservation team and her willingness to mate with Old Yellow, Old Blue produced enough eggs to preserve the species.

◊ Shrek the Sheep: a runaway sheep who evaded capture for six years. When Shrek was eventually caught by musterer Ann Scanlan, the 27 kg fleece he had grown while in hiding was shorn under the bemused gaze of a worldwide TV audience.

◊ Jimmy the Orangutan: Jimmy arrived at Wellington Zoo in 1960, having been rescued from Australia. There, he had been cruelly carted around pubs in an old pram to publicize Wirth's Circus, and by the time Ken Coles, Wellington zookeeper, assumed caregiving duties, Jimmy was addicted to both booze and cigarettes. Coles nursed the red ape back to health, and Jimmy lived for another two years.

◊ Happy Feet: an Antarctic Emperor penguin which became stranded on the Kapiti Coast in June 2011, 4000 km from his home. Happy Feet had ingested sand and twigs and required several operations to clear his stomach. After 10 weeks at Wellington Zoo, Happy Feet sailed on board the research ship Tangaroa and headed for the Campbell Islands. He was shoved overboard to return to the chilly seas, but within a week, his satellite tracker stopped transmitting. Nobody knows whether the silence was because the tracker had fallen off, or whether Happy Feet had become dinner for a whale or leopard seal.

---

6 NATURAL DISASTERS AUCKLANDERS HAVE REASON TO FEAR

The Global Facility for Disaster Reduction and Recovery (funded by the World Bank, the EU and others) has weighed up New Zealand's chances of being struck by a range of natural disasters, and reckons that most of the country lies in harm's way of one form or another. Even Aucklanders have good reason to be kept awake at night ...

◊ Coastal flood: hazard level high – potentially damaging waves are expected to flood the coast at least once in the next 10 years.

◊ Earthquake: hazard level high – there is more than a 20 per cent chance of potentially damaging earthquake shaking in the next 50 years.

◊ Tsunami: hazard level high – there is more than a 20 per cent chance of a potentially damaging tsunami occurring in the next 50 years.

◇ Volcano: hazard level high – Auckland is less than 50 km from a volcano for which a potentially damaging eruption has been recorded in the past 2000 years and future damaging eruptions are possible.

◇ Cyclone: hazard level high – there is more than a 20 per cent chance of potentially damaging wind speeds in the next 10 years.

◇ Wildfire: hazard level high – there is a greater than 50 per cent chance of encountering weather that could support a significant wildfire that is likely to result in loss of both life and property in any given year.

... and 3 things we shouldn't hold our breath for

River flood: hazard level very low – the chance of potentially damaging and life-threatening river floods occurring in the coming 10 years is less than 10 per cent.

Landslide: hazard level very low – the rainfall patterns, terrain slope, geology, soil, land cover and incidence of earthquakes make localized landslides a rare phenomenon.

Water scarcity: Hazard level very low or non-existent – droughts will occur much less than once every 1000 years.

Source: Global Facility for Disaster Reduction and Recovery

9 DISTURBING CHANGES IN NEW ZEALAND'S ATMOSPHERE AND CLIMATE

◇ Levels of CO_2 in the atmosphere are the highest they have been in at least 800,000 years.

◇ Gross greenhouse gas emissions have risen by 24 per cent since 1990, mostly as a result of road transport.

◊ 2016 was New Zealand's hottest year on record, and, in 2019, several locations around the country experienced the driest first half of the year on record.

◊ There were 27 days of extreme UV intensity in 2016.

◊ Production of ozone-depleting substances has dropped by 98 per cent in the last 30 years. The ozone hole is shrinking and is expected to stop forming by the middle of the century.

◊ New Zealand's native and exotic forests removed 67 per cent of our CO_2 emissions.

◊ Our glaciers have lost enough ice to fill 133,000 Olympic-sized swimming pools each year over the past 40 years.

◊ Sea levels have risen 14–22 cm at our four main ports since 1916.

◊ The pH of New Zealand's oceans has decreased in the last 19 years. The increased acidity makes it harder for shellfish to form shells.

Source: *New Zealand's Environmental Reporting Series: Our atmosphere and climate 2017.* Retrieved from www.mfe.govt.nz and www.stats.govt.nz.

5 KIWI-LED GAME-CHANGERS THAT NANOGIRL IS IN LOVE WITH

Nanogirl, Dr Michelle Dickinson's public persona, knows a good thing when she sees one. Her book, *No. 8 Re-Charged*, is filled with riveting manifestations of Kiwi ingenuity.

◊ OnGuard: a system designed to prevent loss of wine from tanks in a strong earthquake. The system works like a shock absorber for the wine tank, allowing the ground beneath the tank to move while the tank itself absorbs the seismic shock.

It prevents wastage of the vintage and has been sold to wineries in California's Napa Valley.

◊ Quiet Revolution: a cylindrical chair that rotates to form a compact circular space equipped with a small desk, power for laptop and mobile phone, and network connections – should you so wish. The environment is enclosed except at the top, and provides a readily accessible silent zone for use in noisy, open-plan offices when you need defence against distraction or other people.

◊ International Volunteer HQ: a Taranaki-based global company that takes the guesswork out of volunteering by vetting projects to ensure they are legitimate, as well as booking flights, sorting out accommodation, advising on inoculation, and providing local knowledge and safety information. So far, 67,000 'voluntourists' have been helped to work on projects in 35 countries.

◊ Allbirds shoes: cosy, supportive shoes made from wool grown in New Zealand and milled in Italy. Because wool wicks away moisture and is antibacterial, the shoes don't smell and are soft enough to be worn without socks. The idea came from Tim Brown, a former All White soccer player, who eventually launched the Allbirds brand with significant US investment.

◊ Flashmate: a small circular device that sits on a cow's rump and, given any indication of a cow's friskiness (for example, a cow's attempt to mate with another cow), flashes red to indicate that the cow is ready for insemination, either natural or artificial. The Flashmate turns green when insemination has been successful. The device costs $8 but can boost the profits on a typical farm by up to $24,000 per annum.

Source: No. 8 Re-charged: 202 world-changing Innovations from New Zealand, by David Downs and Dr Michelle Dickinson (2017, Penguin Books)

3 BUGGY THINGS RUUD KLEINPASTE WOULD LIKE TO SEE IN YOUR GARDEN

◊ Steel-blue ladybirds: they base their menu around aphids in citrus trees, roses, hydrangeas and flax. The larvae are even better than the ladybirds themselves because of their impressive appetite during their growth surge.

◊ Harvestmen (or Daddy Long Legs): they work well at ground level (and just above) to dispatch small slugs and the eggs of the cabbage white butterfly.

◊ Parasitic wasps: one species in particular, *Encarsia formosa,* is adept at dealing with the whitefly on greenhouse tomatoes.

7 NEW ZEALAND PLANTS WITH AN AWESOME REPUTATION IN TRADITIONAL MAORI MEDICINE

◊ Kumarahou *(Pomaderris kumarahou)*: The leaves of this shrub were used by early Maori healers to treat lung conditions, particularly bronchitis and tuberculosis, as well as colds and asthma.

◊ Kawakawa *(Macropiper excelsum)*: The fruit, bark and leaves of this small tree were used to remedy digestive upsets, bloating, cramping, circulation problems, pain and inflammation.

◊ Manuka *(Leptospermum scoparium)*: Manuka (tea tree) oil is anti-inflammatory, anti-microbial, and anti-fungal. The leaves, seeds and bark were used in poultices and ointments to treat burns and scalds, ringworm and eczema. Ashes of manuka were rubbed on the scalp to cure dandruff.

◊ Koromiko *(Hebe salicifolia, H. stricta)*: The unopened buds and young leaves of this ornamental plant were used in the treatment of diarrhoea and as a tonic, also to help heal skin infections and ulcers.

◊ Harakeke *(Phormium tenax)*: The flax plant used widely, from treating constipation to healing burns as well as and gunshot and bayonet wounds.

◊ Tutu *(Coriaria arborea)*: Maori had numerous uses for tutu, a poisonous plant that can be made into an ointment to use in the treatment of arthritis, skin rashes and gout.

◊ Totara *(Podocarpus totara)*: Totara is naturally anti-microbial and has been discovered to help with cases of *Staphylococcus* aureus infection that are unresponsive to pharmaceutical antibiotics.

---

15 PLANTS THAT PROMPT CALLS TO THE NATIONAL POISONS CENTRE

Eat them, brush up against them or inhale their sawdust – and you might be in trouble. New Zealand has a number of poisonous plants that spark panicky phone calls to the New Zealand National Poisons Centre in Dunedin. Reactions range from the relatively mild (nausea, vomiting, diarrhoea, anorexia, malaise, fever, headache and/or sweating) to the downright deadly (hallucinations, delirium, drowsiness, ataxia, blurred vision, slurred speech, weakness, paraesthesia, facial numbness or paralysis, coma and respiratory muscle weakness, with risk of respiratory failure). Combined, black nightshade and the Arum lily account for almost half of all the calls.

Black nightshade	*Solanum nigrum*
Arum lily	*Zantedeschia aethiopica*
Kowhai	*Sophora spp.*
Euphorbia	*Euphorbia spp.*
Peace lily	*Spathiphyllum spp.*
Agapanthus	*Agapanthus spp.*

Stinking iris	*Iris foetidissima*
Rhubarb	*Rheum rhabarbarum*
Taro	*Colocasia esculentum*
Daffodil	*Narcissus spp.*
Oleander	*Nerium oleander*
Hemlock	*Conium maculatum*
Karaka	*Corynocarpus laevigatus*
Ongaonga	*Urtica ferox*
Foxglove	*Digitalis purpurea*

Source: NZ National Poisons Centre, Dunedin

SHAME ON US: 12 NATURAL ENEMIES OF NEW ZEALAND

Introduced species that have wreaked havoc on native birds, animals, fish, and forests:

Humans	Cats
Possums	Rats
Deer	Goats
Stoats	Pigs
Ferrets	Wasps
Weasels	Hedgehogs

STARRY, STARRY NIGHTS:
THE 7 MOST REWARDING PLACES FOR GAZING INTO THE NIGHT SKY

No, don't bother looking for heavenly bodies on K Road in Auckland late on a Friday night. You need a location where light pollution won't dim your view of a celestial panorama.

◊ Tekapo: the observatory on top of Mt John (in the International Dark Sky Reserve)

◊ Twizel: in the hot tub at Ashley Mackenzie Villa and Spa

◊ Aoraki/Mt Cook: the Hillary Deck at the Alpine Centre

◊ Queenstown: at the top of the Skyline Gondola

◊ Wairarapa: Stonehenge Aotearoa

◊ Stewart Island

◊ The Catlins Coast, in the southeastern corner of the South Island.

LOOK UP! 3 HEAVENLY EVENTS
THAT WILL BE WORTH THE WAIT

◊ A rare conjunction between Jupiter and Saturn will occur on 21 December 2020. The two planets will pass by each other, appearing to make a 'double star' in the sky.

◊ A bright new 'star' will appear in the constellation Cygnus, due to a supernova in the year 2022.

◊ A partial solar eclipse, best visible from southern New Zealand, will occur on 21 September 2025.

9 PROFESSIONAL TIPS FOR TRAINING A GREAT SHEEPDOG

◊ Dogs are not born with bad habits. We let them develop and are then faced with the problem of dealing with them.

◊ Be firm but fair. Repetition and consistency are key. Recognize and reward progress.

◊ Training is all about getting your dog to conform. If your dog conforms to your wishes, you will train it.

◊ Training should be a process where each step follows logically from the one before and prepares the dog for the one that comes next.

◊ Before you can train your dog, it needs to exhibit a genuine desire to work stock.

◊ The 'puppy stage' (from 8 weeks to 8 months) is very important. Bonding, building respect and impressing upon your young dog the need to conform are priorities at this stage.

◊ Successful training requires the dog to be confident in its desire and interest to work sheep. Every command you teach

your dog can take away a little of its initiative, so build up a good base before commencing training and maintain it throughout your program.

◊ The two most important commands are an effective 'wayleggo' (an abbreviation of 'come away and let them go', used when you want the dog to come back to you) and 'stop'. These commands give you control of your dog, and, if you have control of your dog, it becomes easy to control your stock.

◊ Always remember: It is too easy to blame the dog for your own shortcomings.

Source: Lloyd Smith, author of *Pup Pen to Paddock: A no-nonsense guide to rearing and training better sheep dogs*

---

11 New Zealand beaches
where fatal shark attacks have occurred

◊ Wellington Harbour (1852)

◊ Kumara, West Coast (1896)

◊ Marine Parade, Napier (1896)

◊ Moeraki (1907, 1967)

◊ St Clair, Dunedin (1964)

◊ Manukau Harbour, Auckland (1966)

◊ Oakura, Taranaki (1966)

◊ St Kilda, Dunedin (1967)

◊ Aramoana, Dunedin (1968)

◊ Te Kaha, Bay of Plenty (1976)

◊ Muriwai, Auckland (2013)

Hot dogs!
9 of New Zealand's favourite canines

◊ Hairy Maclary, from Donaldson's Dairy

◊ Hercules, the huntaway cross that starred in the Toyota 'Bugger' advertisements

◊ Caesar the bulldog, A Company, 4 Battalion, New Zealand Rifle Brigade, who helped rescue wounded troops during the Battle of the Somme in 1916

◊ Dog, hero of the *Footrot Flats* cartoon strip

◊ Minstrel, the black-and-white sheepdog who was the constant companion of poet Sam Hunt

◊ Paddy, the wire-haired fox terrier who played Wilson in the original Lotto ads

◊ Spot, the Jack Russell terrier who starred in Telecom advertising through the 90s

◊ The bronze statue of a sheepdog outside the Church of the Good Shepherd, Lake Tekapo

◊ Watchman the beagle, a long-serving sniffer dog at Auckland Airport, now retired.

6 Kiwi scientists who couldn't
mansplain even if they tried

◊ Beatrice Tinsley was light years ahead of most scientists in New Zealand. An astronomer and cosmologist, she studied the evolution of galaxies and, in 1978, she became the first female professor of astronomy at Yale University. Many believe she was in line for a Nobel Prize before her death at the age of just 40. A play about her life was entitled *Bright*

Star, and in December 2010 the New Zealand Geographic Board officially named a mountain after her in Fiordland's Kepler Mountains.

◊ Michelle Dickinson developed her alter ego 'Nanogirl' as a way of conquering her shyness and fear of public speaking. Her avowed intention is to explain science, technology and engineering in a way that makes complex subject matter worthy of widespread admiration and interest. She is a senior lecturer in chemical and material engineering at Auckland University, and runs New Zealand's only nanomechanical testing lab.

◊ Siouxsie Wiles is a microbiologist whose specialist areas are infectious diseases and bioluminescence. She is passionate about demystifying science for the general public and makes regular media appearances to discuss science stories in the news. Her book *Antibiotic Resistance: The End of Modern Medicine* was published in 2017 and discussed the growing worldwide problem of resistance to antibiotics.

◊ Margaret Brimble is known internationally for her work synthesising bioactive natural products and novel peptides with wide-ranging applications; in other words, she discovers new drugs to treat disease. She recently discovered a drug to treat females who have Rett Syndrome, and is currently working on developing a vaccine to protect against melanoma. Among her many accolades, she was awarded the Rutherford Medal in 2012 by the Royal Society of New Zealand.

◊ Rosemary Askin is a geologist who, at the age of 21, became the first New Zealand woman to undertake her own research programme in Antarctica. Her 1970 expedition resulted in the discovery of Antarctica's richest-known site of fossilized fish remains. In 1982, she was part of a research team that discovered the first mammal fossils in Antarctica, and she was involved in research that demonstrated that Antarctica experienced an abrupt warming cycle 15 million years ago.

◊ Vicki Hyde is a science writer and editor. Her 2006 book, *Oddzone: Paranormal phenomena, alien abductions, animal mysteries, psychics and mediums and other weird Kiwi stuff*, discussed whether ancient Celts, Egyptians or Vikings discovered Aotearoa before Maori, and whether the phantom canoe seen by Guide Sophia on Lake Tarawera shortly before a volcanic eruption was an ill omen. She was 'chair-entity' (that's the society's little joke) of the New Zealand Skeptics society from 1997-2010. In 2013, she arranged for *Sensing Murder* psychic Sue Nicholson to speak at the society's annual conference about her 21 years of experiences as a psychic medium.

The 10 worst nightmares of Kiwi greenies

◊ Genetic engineering

◊ Plastic in oceans

◊ Diesel emissions

◊ Nuclear weapons

◊ Deep-sea drilling

◊ Cellphone towers

◊ Toxic chemicals

◊ Air pollution

◊ Destruction of native forests

◊ Greenhouse gas emissions.

7 LESSONS THAT SURPRISED A THIRD-YEAR STUDENT AT AUCKLAND MED SCHOOL

◊ Men have a longer urethra than women, and can therefore hold their pee for longer.

◊ Cigarette smoking is a protective factor against ulcerative colitis. The nicotine suppresses the immune response and thus reduces inflammation. The chemicals in smoke may also increase mucus production in the part of the colon where ulcerative colitis starts.

◊ Gynaecomastia (the development of breasts in boys) is surprisingly common.

◊ Slog is inevitable. You have to rote learn a whole lot of stuff before you can start pulling it all together.

◊ There's a reason Crocs are popular footwear among medical teams. Wearing dress shoes on ward rounds means sore feet and maybe even plantar fasciitis.

◊ Most med school students went to Auckland Grammar School, St Kentigern's or Kings College.

◊ Very often, Wikipedia and YouTube videos explain things more clearly than the lecturers do.

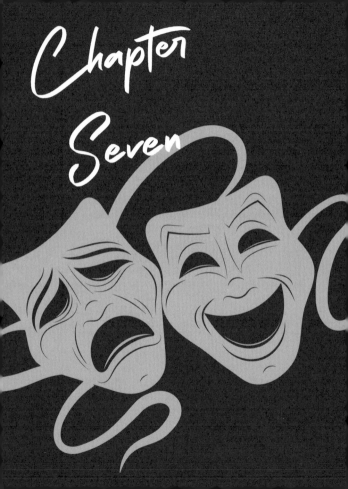

Chapter

Seven

ARTS and ENTERTAINMENT:
Character Studies

DAYS THAT CHANGED NEW ZEALAND

25 May 1992: Shortland Street *premieres*

It wasn't supposed to last. In fact, less than flattering reviews would have seen *Shortland Street* swiftly euthanized if TVNZ hadn't optimistically ordered a year's worth of episodes in advance. But the country's homegrown medical melodrama clings to life and starts to hit its stride. It develops a reputation for reflecting the society around it – even anticipating social changes – and gives hundreds of Kiwi actors a chance of regular employment. By the time the show is 25 years old, 40 per cent of the nation's TV viewers will have a regular appointment with the doctors each weekday night.

NAME THAT TUNE: THE OPENING LINES OF 11 CLASSIC KIWI SONGS

◊ Through falling leaves I pick my way slowly ('Nature' – The Fourmyula)

◊ Hey, I got a lot of faith in you ('Slice of Heaven' – Dave Dobbyn)

◊ When I was a young boy ('Six Months in a Leaky Boat' – Split Enz)

◊ I'm tired of the city life ('April Sun in Cuba' – Dragon)

- ◊ I look at the sunrise ('Counting the Beat' - The Swingers)

- ◊ Don't stray, don't ever go away ('Sway' - Bic Runga)

- ◊ I can't remember last time I thanked you
  ('Loyal' - Dave Dobbyn)

- ◊ Brother Pele's in the back, Sweet Zina's in the front
  ('How Bizarre' - OMC)

- ◊ There is freedom within, there is freedom without
  ('Don't Dream It's Over' - Crowded House)

- ◊ I've never seen a diamond in the flesh ('Royals' - Lorde)

- ◊ E Ihowa Atua, O nga iwi matou ra (God Defend New Zealand)

---

6 REASONS TIM WILSON'S BOW TIE
MAKES HIM A BRILLIANT BROADCASTER

- ◊ Anyone with the aptitude for tying a bow correctly has to be patient and intelligent; in other words, he's bound to be a good listener.

- ◊ Tying a bow tie properly shows commitment to an art form.

- ◊ Successfully pairing a bow tie with a shirt requires elevated aesthetic awareness.

- ◊ Wearing a bow tie well signposts a meticulous nature and great attention to detail, so his stories are likely to be comprehensive and trustworthy.

- ◊ James Bond wore one, and he was always cool and in control. (After the release of any new Bond film, sales of bowties surge.) When Tim does goofy, he's just kidding.

- ◊ Doesn't a bow tie imply that there is a gift waiting to be unwrapped?

NATIONAL SELFIES: 9 FAMOUS PHOTOGRAPHS

◊ The Maori Battalion performing a haka for the King of Greece, at Helwan, Egypt, during World War II. Wearing uniforms of army shorts, shirts with rolled-up sleeves, knee socks and leather boots, performers are caught in mid-air. Each soldier carries a thin spear with pointed ends, and footprints are clear in the desert sands. The photo is the cover of a book called *Ake Ake Kia Kaha E!: Forever Brave*, Wira Gardiner's history of B Company 28 (Maori) Battalion.

◊ The portrait of Michael Joseph Savage by Spencer Digby. The 1930s black-and-white photograph of the Labour Party prime minister wearing round glasses and a quiet smile quickly became a New Zealand icon. After Savage died in 1940, homes everywhere would proudly hang a print of it.

◊ Tenzing Norgay at the summit of Mt Everest, photographed by Sir Ed Hillary on 29 May 1953. Given Sir Ed's inclination for modesty, it is not surprising the famous photo proving the first successful summit of the world's highest mountain does not show the mountain's conqueror, but rather, his Sherpa companion.

◊ Whina Cooper with her mokopuna, three-year-old Irene Cooper, on 14 September 1975, as they set off from the far north on the hikoi to Wellington. Photographed from the back by Michael Tubberty, Cooper is wearing her customary head scarf, a cardigan and a long black skirt. In her right hand she holds a walking stick; in her left, she holds her granddaughter's hand. A gravel road stretches ahead.

◊ 'Monsoon Girl', by Brian Brake. One image from Brake's photo essay that was published in *Life* magazine in 1961, the sensuous portrait of an Indian girl in a red sari, turning her face up to receive the monsoon raindrops, was a set-up. Brake had asked an actress to pose on a terrace, telling her to 'feel the rain', as the contents of a large watering can cascaded over her face.

◊ Ruby and Bella, the twin daughters of Mike Hosking, photographed just before Christmas 2002 by Simon Runting in Newmarket, Auckland. Deeply peeved by the photograph's publication in *New Idea* magazine, Mike Hosking launched a court case on the grounds of invasion of privacy. But a high court judge rejected the case, saying: 'Mr Hosking has deliberately courted publicity both before and after the children's birth and he necessarily sacrifices, to a greater or lesser degree, the privacy ordinarily enjoyed by those who are not household names'.

◊ *'Hemi and Rebecca know better how to smoke cigarettes',* by Ans Westra. Two young children light their 'cigarettes' – rolled-up Minties wrappers – from a small piece of burning wood as they stand in front of an old cooker. The photo is one of 44 images published as *Washday at the Pa*. The Maori Women's Welfare League complained that the image depicted a 'non-average' (i.e. poor) Maori family, and controversy erupted when the Minister of Education ordered all copies of the book destroyed. The book was defiantly republished by Caxton Press a year later, with 22 additional photos.

◊ 'Avery Jackson', Robin Hammond's image of a nine-year-old transgender girl, made the cover of *National Geographic's* January 2017 special issue on gender. Avery, wearing a pink T-shirt and pants, and with her hair dyed pink, looks proudly and directly at the camera. She is the first transgender person to appear on the magazine's cover. Hammond has won four Amnesty International awards for human rights journalism.

◊ Jacinda Ardern, wearing a hijab, embracing Somali-born Naima Abdi at a wreath-laying at Wellington's Kilbirnie Mosque on 17 March 2019. The iconic image of empathy was captured by Wellington photographer Hagen Hopkins for Getty Images and beamed out from the Burj Khalifa, an 829-metre-tall skyscraper in Dubai.

9 BOOKS SET IN NEW ZEALAND BUT NOT WRITTEN BY KIWIS

The Christmas Oratorio, a novel by Swedish author Göran Tunström, published in 1983.

Cloud Atlas, a 2004 novel by British author David Mitchell, which begins in the Chatham Islands in 1850.

The Colour, a 2003 novel by Rose Tremain, set during the gold rush.

Erewhon: or, Over the Range, a novel by Samuel Butler, based on Butler's own experiences of working on a sheep farm in the 1860s.

Generation A, a novel from Canadian novelist Douglas Coupland, which includes a main character from Palmerston North.

In Search of the Castaways, (in French: *Les Enfants du capitaine Grant*), an adventure story by French writer Jules Verne, published in 1867.

The Snow Tiger, a 2002 novel by English author Desmond Bagley, set in a small mining community following an avalanche.

Two Years' Vacation (in French: *Deux ans de vacances*), an adventure novel by Jules Verne.

The Witch's Thorn, a 1951 novel by Australian author Ruth Park, is set in the fictional North Island town of Te Kana.

5 CRINGY ANSWERS MISS UNIVERSE NZ FINALISTS HAVE GIVEN DURING INTERVIEWS

◊ I think 'beauty on the inside' is just being 100 per cent naturally organic.

◊ I think you need to set your mindset right when you go into this journey and if you take this journey for the journey, well

- ◊ then, I guess you've accomplished something that you want to do, but if you do take this journey and you want to win, well then, there's a bonus for you as well.

- ◊ Miss Universe NZ has made me lot more confident as a person. I am now, you know, not afraid to go out in the community and talk to people and do one of my many bake sales. I've also gotten quite good at making Afghan biscuits.

- ◊ I don't think I'd want to meet Donald Trump. I really don't appreciate his views, especially on the transgender community. I have a lot of LGBTQI friends.

- ◊ I guess when you bring in children's pageants and you bring in stereotypes, that is where you can get some bad reputation.

---

10 CHEESY ROMANCE TITLES BY NEW ZEALAND AUTHORS

- ◊ *Beguile Me Not,* by Odelia Floris (CreateSpace Independent Publishing Platform, 2015)

- ◊ *Brooding Billionaire, Impoverished Princess,* by Robyn Donald (Mills & Boon, 2010)

- ◊ *Christmas with Dr Delicious,* by Sue Mackay (Mills & Boon, 2012)

- ◊ *Claiming His Convenient Fiancée,* by Natalie Anderson (Mills & Boon, 2017)

- ◊ *Falling for Her Fake Fiancé,* by Sue Mackay (Mills & Boon, 2017)

- ◊ *Rich, Ruthless and Secretly Royal,* by Robyn Donald (Mills & Boon, 2009)

- ◊ *Talking Dirty with the CEO,* by Jackie Ashenden (Entangled Publishing, 2013)

- ◊ *The Determined Virgin,* by Daphne Clair (Mills & Boon, 2014)

- ◊ *The Mediterranean Prince's Captive Virgin,* by Robyn Donald (Mills & Boon, 2011)

- ◊ *Unbuttoned by Her Maverick Boss,* by Natalie Anderson (Mills & Boon, 2010)

The 9 tallest Kiwi actors, and where you might have seen them

- ◊ Luke Bilbrough, 193 cm: bar punter in *Westside,* Series 3

- ◊ Paul Norell, 193 cm: King of the Dead in *Lord of the Rings: The Return of the King*

- ◊ Bradley Hagan, 193 cm: posh waiter in *Filthy Rich,* Series 1

- ◊ Fraser McLeod, 194 cm: soldier in the feature film *Home for Christmas*

- ◊ Lincoln Jackson, 195 cm: Hugo Horton in Waiheke Island Theatre's production of *The Vicar of Dibley*

- ◊ Oliver Driver, 198 cm: Eggther the Giant, in *The Almighty Johnsons,* Series 2

- ◊ Alex Board, 200 cm: Friar Laurence in St Kentigern College's production of *Romeo and Juliet* in 2008

- ◊ Bruce Spence, 201 cm: Jedediah the pilot in *Mad Max 3: Beyond Thunderdome*

- ◊ Paul Randall, 216 cm: a large-scale double in *The Hobbit*

10 DESCRIPTIONS OF SAM HUNT

Sam Hunt's physical attributes – his woolly hair, his long, skinny legs, his gravelly voice – have provoked as much reaction, acclaim, even, as his poems. There's no mistaking Sam for anybody else. So firmly has he maintained his idiosyncratic style that we've become quite accustomed to it … fond of it, even. In the mid-80s, Sam migrated from *Metro* magazine's 'Worst Dressed' List one year to their 'Best Dressed List' the next – without, he noted, even changing his shirt.

As a man, he remains at once familiar and yet remote, staunchly defending his personal privacy while striving for the widest possible audience for his work. The contradictions are part of his legend. As much as we think we can define him, we will never really know him. His poetry, thankfully, is accessible to anyone who will listen.

◊ 'I was intrigued by the tall, gangling, mop-haired boy who stood on the doorstep that day in November 1964. He looked like a mixture of cavalier, pirate, sixth form boy, and Dr Who.' – Meg Campbell

◊ 'In recital his voice is memorable. It evokes at one and the same time a wheezing harmonica and a raucous seagull. With bouffant hairdo like an exploded wool bale, bony bangle-clad wrists and fingers restlessly in motion, this is the poet as rock 'n' roller, affirming the power of performance.' – Aotearoa New Zealand Poetry Archive

◊ 'Hunt's laugh is frequent and slightly pained, as if he's being kicked repeatedly in the funny bone. In between, he throws out a protective wall of interference - anecdotes, quotes and poems - that you can never quite see behind.' – Diana Wichtel

◊ 'A travelling roadshow of man, dog and bottle.' – Elizabeth Caffin, in the *Oxford History of New Zealand Literature*

◊ 'His swearing and sometimes devilish laughter reminds you that the romantic and soulful scribe can be a brambly and cantankerous character.' – Paulette Crowley, Stuff

◊ '... we'd often spot his unmistakable figure striding along the roadside: tall and thin, shock-headed and long-legged, clad rakishly in stovepipe jeans and flowing scarves, with his equally famous sheepdog Minstrel loping at his heels.' – Meg Mundell, Cordite Poetry Review

◊ 'A lot of his poems come out of loneliness, not the pleasant kind of thing called solitude, but loneliness. He has a price to pay for his kind of life.' – Jill McCracken, Landfall

◊ '… as clown, orator, poet-preacherman, he dances out all our agonies in public.' – Gary McCormick

◊ 'A rollicking, rambunctious raconteur and unreformed pot head' – Howard Davis, Scoop

◊ 'After five minutes of conversing, you feel as if you want to, if not have his babies, then perhaps volunteer that your sister do so.' – Tim Wilson, Quote Unquote

7 SADNESSES IN THE LIFE OF KIRI TE KANAWA

◊ Cookbook author Digby Law published a book in August 1978 entitled A Vegetable Cookbook. Among the 400 recipes were instructions for a dish called Kiri Te Kumara. It involved baking kumara with a coating of butter, brown sugar, mace, salt and the grated rind of an orange. After half an hour or so, the topping on the kumara would reportedly turn into a pleasing, brown, gooey mess.

◊ In a 1989 book called Angel Gear, the story of a Sam Hunt poetry tour chronicled by Colin Hogg, Hunt recalls meeting the operatic diva: 'She taught me how to save my throat, use my chest. Don't like her tunes – great arse, though', observed the unchivalrous poet.

◊ In 1997, while she was rehearsing in Brazil, her husband, Desmond Park, is said to have informed her by telegram that, after 30 years of marriage, he was leaving her. She has claimed she can't remember the details of how, exactly, the break-up was sprung upon her, but told the *Telegraph* newspaper in the UK, 'I prefer just to let it go because it's not important. I think that what is important is that I don't look as sad as I was.'

◊ When she was a few weeks old, she was adopted by a Maori father and an Irish mother and never attempted to trace her natural parents, believing that it might somehow end in grief. In 1998, her instinct proved correct. One of her half-brothers, Jim Rawstron, contacted her and, reluctantly, she agreed to a reunion. When the story found its way into the newspapers, Dame Kiri felt she had been betrayed. 'I thought I had found somebody I could hold on to', she noted sadly. 'I'll never trust such a thing again. I am not interested.'

◊ In 2007, Te Kanawa was due to share the stage for a series of concerts with Australian singer John Farnham. Tickets were already selling well when Kiri learned that it was commonplace for middle-aged women in the audience to whip off their knickers and fling them on stage for Farnham to scoop up and display. Aghast at the thought of such indignities, the Kiwi soprano pulled out of the deal. She ended up in court as a result, with the event-management company attempting to sue her for breach of contract.

◊ Despite periodically voicing an interest in taking on acting roles, the appearance for which she was most obviously suited – that of Australian opera star Dame Nellie Melba in the BBC drama *Downton Abbey* – was ungraciously slammed by Rupert Christiansen, the *Telegraph's* opera critic. 'Dame Kiri delivered a few lines of dialogue in stiffly parroted and nervous fashion, which reminded me that even in her glorious vocal prime she had never been much of an actress … I greatly admire the shrewd casting of *Downton Abbey*, but this was not one of its happier inspirations', he sniffed.

◊ In 2017, while announcing her retirement from singing in public, Kiri revealed on the BBC's *Today* program that the one accolade she had never received was self-approval. 'I never actually came off stage saying, "I've really nailed it". Never. I always thought there was a mistake in it.'

5 THINGS LORDE HAS SAID ABOUT OTHER SINGERS

◊ On Lana Del Ray: '... it's so unhealthy for girls to be listening to, you know, "I'm nothing without you". This sort of shirt-tugging, desperate, "don't leave me" stuff. That's not a good thing for young girls, even young people, to hear.'

◊ On David Bowie: 'David was different. I'll never forget the caressing of our hands as we spoke, or the light in his eyes … That night something changed in me … I realized I was proud of my spiky strangeness because he had been proud of his.'

◊ On Beyoncé: 'Beyoncé is a goddess and a superhuman performer and the epitome of poise and grace. Why would I dislike Beyoncé? I don't even know if it's possible.'

◊ On Lou Reed: 'Lou Reed taught me that unflinching honesty is a very powerful tool in songwriting.'

◊ On Selena Gomez: 'I'm a feminist, and the theme of her song is "When you're ready, come and get it from me". I'm sick of women being portrayed this way.'

… and 5 things she said about herself

◊ 'Songwriting is selfish. I make music for myself, using it as an outlet, something to fulfil my creative desires – yet the rewards of deciding to write something can keep an artist going for a lifetime, can whip me across datelines, throw me under lights.'

◊ 'Adults like to ask me how I'm coping with things, because adults are always nervous there's a looming breakdown on the horizon, I guess.'

◊ 'I'm not a spreadsheet with hair; will never be. I am an artist, an author, with a hunger for showing people what I can do and a talent for making people turn my name into a call while they're waiting front row.'

◊ 'When I was a kid I thought big records had to be made a certain way - to be sterile and calculated in craft; that something had to be sacrificed. I have had the divine thrill of disproving that first hand, twice over.'

◊ 'The hard thing was when people would ask me: "Do you feel 16?" and I'm like: "I don't know, I've never been 40".'

---

12 CAFÉS OFFERING BETTER THAN AVERAGE CHANCES OF BUMPING INTO A KIWI SINGER-SONGWRITER

The strategy for sighting caffeine-addicted musos is relatively straightforward, thanks to a survey conducted by the Australasian Performing Right Association (APRA). In January 2015, APRA released a ranking of New Zealand postcodes, based on how many of their members lived in each location. If we assume that singer-songwriters aren't rich enough to shift to bigger, better homes all that often, and if we assume that they don't want to travel too far for their flat whites and long blacks, it's possible to pinpoint places where the chances are better than average that you will find them hanging out.

◊ Grey Lynn/Kingsland: Kokako Café in Grey Lynn; Mondays in Kingsland

◊ Newtown/Brooklyn: Brooklyn Deli

◊ Mt Eden/Three Kings: Olaf's Artisan Bakery Cafe or the Return of Rad, both in Mt Eden

◊ Te Aro/Mt Victoria, Wellington: Fidel's Café on Cuba Street, or Peoples Coffee Café, Newtown

◊ Auckland Central/Grafton: Hum Salon or the Welcome Eatery in Grafton, or Remedy Coffee in Wellesley Street

◊ Ponsonby: Orphan's Kitchen or Little Bird Unbakery

◊ Titirangi/Green Bay: Deco Eatery in Titirangi

◊ Sandringham: Petit Bocal

◊ Mt Albert/New Lynn/Blockhouse Bay: L'Oeuf in Mt Albert, the Old Woodshop & Corner Café in New Lynn

◊ Western Springs/Westmere/Point Chevalier: Garnet Station in Westmere

◊ Onehunga: The Cozy Cafeteria

◊ Wanganui: Mud Ducks Café

Chapter Eight

SPORTS and LEISURE:

Fun and Games

DAYS THAT CHANGED NEW ZEALAND

26 June 1987: AJ Hackett bungy jumps off the Eiffel Tower

After three months of planning and an awful lot of subterfuge, AJ Hackett has outfoxed security officials and spent the night high up inside the Eiffel Tower, hiding inside a sleeping bag. At first light this morning, wearing a greenstone pendant and a tuxedo, AJ Hackett leaps 100 metres off this most recognizable of buildings. Camera crews beam the images to audiences around the world. AJ is immediately arrested but released within five minutes. Bungy-jumping has just made its international debut. New Zealand quickly becomes the destination for anyone who fancies strapping rubber bands to their ankles and leaping into the void – and forever more, the country is recognized as the home of adventure tourism.

6 BAD KIWI SPORTS JOKES

◊ What's the difference between New Zealand and a tea bag? The tea bag stays in the cup longer.

◊ Why aren't the New Zealand football team allowed to own a dog? Because they can't hold on to a lead.

◊ Why does New Zealand have some of the fastest racehorses in the world? Because the horses have seen what they do with their sheep.

◊ What time does Marina Erakovic go to bed? Tennish.

◊ Why do Kiwis make better lovers than the Aussies? Because Kiwis are the only ones who can stay on top for 45 minutes and still come second.

◊ What's the difference between Cinderella and the New Zealand rugby team? Cinderella wanted to get to the ball.

LYDIA KO'S 5 FAVOURITE GOLF COURSES

◊ Cypress Point Club, California: I love the ocean views and the seals ... a place like no other!

◊ Jack's Point, Queenstown: A stunning blend of mountains and the ocean views.

◊ The Hills Golf Club, Arrowtown: I love all the variations of the hills on the golf course and the unique art statues.

◊ Gulf Harbour Country Club: It was my home club for a long time, and I love the views.

◊ Lake Merced Golf Club, California: I won my first LPGA tournament as an LPGA member here. I love the tricky elements of the golf course, and the fact that the course is always in great condition.

Source: Lydia Ko

10 NATIONAL TEAMS WITH 'BLACK' IN THEIR NAME

◊ All Blacks — Men's rugby union

◊ Black Ferns — Women's rugby union

◊ Black Caps — Men's cricket

◊ Black Sox — Men's softball

◊ Black Sticks — Men's and women's field hockey

◊ Ice Blacks — Men's ice hockey

◊ Tall Blacks — Men's basketball

◊ Wheel Blacks — Wheelchair rugby

◊ Black Fins — Surf lifesaving

◊ Iron Blacks — American football or gridiron

... and one no longer used

For a few months, the men's badminton team adopted the name Black Cocks, until the international Badminton Federation poured cold water over the ribald humour and the name was officially dropped.

... and one whose potential should be explored

Why doesn't the NZ golf team consider calling itself the Black Holes?

10 THINGS KIWI NUDISTS SHOULD NEVER DO

Alan MacDiarmid was a nudist, and that didn't stop him winning a Nobel prize in chemistry. Nevertheless, even he would have acknowledged there are some things you should never do in your natural state.

◊ Practise your Cossack dancing

◊ Prune roses

◊ Fry bacon and eggs

◊ Sit on a leather car seat on a hot summer's day

◊ Hop over a barbed-wire fence

◊ Join in a vigorous game of beach volleyball

◊ Play Twister

◊ Tend beehives

◊ Open the door to the Uber Eats driver

◊ Ask a policeman for directions

NEW ZEALAND'S 6 MOST SUCCESSFUL OLYMPIC SPORTS

Since Kiwis first started competing as an exclusively New Zealand team, the tally of Olympic medals has risen to 123. Only three of these medals have been won at the Winter Games, the two most recent being in February 2018. Our most successful Olympic sports are:

No. of medals	Sport	Gold count
24	Rowing	11
24	Athletics	10
22	Sailing	9
12	Canoeing	7
10	Equestrian	3
8	Cycling	1

11 INGLORIOUS MOMENTS IN NEW ZEALAND'S SPORTING HISTORY

It seems we will never get over the notorious Underarm Incident, so harshly did it engrave itself on our national sporting psyche. On 16 July 2005, the Beige Brigade, cricket's fervent and flamboyant supporters, even paid out $10,000 on a TradeMe auction to secure one of the two cricket balls used in the infamous incident at the Melbourne Cricket Ground back in 1981. But cricket is not the only sport to have been tainted with something less than marvellousness, as these infamous occasions demonstrate:

◊ On 28 March 1955, playing England at Eden Park, the New Zealand cricket team is all out for 26 runs. The match didn't start too badly. In the first innings, the Kiwis had scored 200 and dismissed England for 246. But in the second innings, English bowler Bob Appleyard takes four for seven; Brian Statham, three for nine; and Frank Tyson, two for 10. Bert Sutcliffe is the only one to make it to double figures, with a score of 11.

◊ On 25 July 1981, Waikato are preparing to take on the Springboks at Rugby Park in Hamilton when hundreds of protesters invade the pitch just before kick-off. The police and the protesters are pelted with bottles and stones by fans, but the ground is eventually cleared. Then word comes in that Pat McQuarrie, a World War II Spitfire pilot, has stolen a light plane and is heading for the stadium. He's a fan of a good game but detests apartheid and is already a veteran of the flour-bomb style of protest. As concern rises over crowd control, the police squad's hand is effectively forced by the unseen aviator, and the game is cancelled.

◊ On 3 April 1989, Paul Holmes premieres his new current affairs programme on television. Dennis Conner, the America's Cup skipper, is invited for an interview. Holmes needles Conner, suggesting he might wish to apologize to the country for describing Kiwi yacht designer Bruce Farr as 'full of shit'. Conner's eyes turn steely grey and his face sets hard. 'I have to run now. Thank you very much for having me', he snarls, before storming off the set.

◊ In December 2000, Gary Fisken, 'Sock' O'Connell and Paul Jackson present a 14.35 kg snapper in order to claim $20,000 prize money at the Matamata Fishing Club contest. However, the fish appears disconcertingly droopy. Fisken is adamant that he caught the fish legitimately, but later, a food technologist examines the fish and concludes it has been dead for about two weeks. The three fishermen are charged with cheating. Although later cleared by a judge who says the evidence from the post-mortem was unreliable, the fishermen are denied the prize money and banned from future contests.

◊ On 4 November 2002, Dave Walden of the BlackHeart campaign flutters a 'Staunch and True' banner down at the America's Cup Village. The campaign has been spawned by the so-called treachery of Russell Coutts and Brad Butterworth in deciding to jump waka and sail for Ernesto Bertarelli's Swiss syndicate Alinghi. Intimidation and threats of violence are unleashed against the sailors' families, although Blackheart spokespeople deny the criminal behaviour originates from its membership.

◊ On 15 November 2003: 'Four more years, boys, four more years'. As the whistle blows at the end of the match that the Australians have won 22–10, George Gregan, the Australian captain, taunts the All Blacks over their third loss in a semi-final in five Rugby World Cups.

◊ On 7 July 2006, an Australian advertisement promoting a Tri-Nations test between New Zealand and Australia shows the All Blacks performing the haka carrying computer-generated handbags. The image refers to the earlier altercation in a Christchurch pub in which Tana Umaga hit Chris Masoe over the head with a handbag, hard enough to smash the mobile phone it contained.

◊ On 20 July 2011, just when everything seemed to be going so well, Tiger Williams pulls the plug on his relationship with his Kiwi caddy, Steve Williams. Williams discovers his loyalty through all of Tiger's scandals has apparently been for nought. 'After 13 years of loyal service, needless to say this came as a shock,' says Williams.

◊ On 17 August 2011, Telecom premieres an advertising campaign asking All Black supporters to abstain from sex during the Rugby World Cup. Within two days, Telecom apologises to disgruntled rugby fans unable to endure the sight of Sean Fitzpatrick driving a pink bumper car while exhorting All Black supporters to sacrifice sex for six weeks. 'Full credit to the opposition,' says Telecom. 'We listened to your views, and we have acted quickly to change our game plan.'

◊ On 18 September 2013, America's Cup racing is on in San Francisco, and Dean Barker has sailed Team New Zealand to an 8-1 lead in the 'best of 17' series. The America's Cup's return to New Zealand seems assured. And yet, in the post-racing press conference, Jimmy Spittle delivers a witheringly trenchant observation: 'I think the question is: imagine if these guys lost from here. What an upset that would be.' His Team Oracle peel off 8 straight wins to win the regatta 9-8 and retain the prized piece of silverware. Dean Barker – and Kiwi hopes – are shattered.

◊ On 1 July 2014, Cricketer Lou Vincent issues a video statement admitting to match fixing. 'My name is Lou Vincent and I am a cheat,' he states. 'I have abused my position as a professional sportsman on a number of occasions by choosing to accept money through fixing. I have shamed my country. I have shamed my sport. I have shamed those close to me. For that, I am not proud.' Vincent is banned for life from any further involvement in the sport.

---

14 MASCOTS THAT ATTEND THE MITRE 10 CUP RUGBY TEAMS

The Taniwha (Northland)

The Harbour Master (North Harbour)

Seagull (Auckland)

Steely Dan (Counties Manukau)

Mooloo the Cow (Waikato)

Hori BOP (Bay of Plenty)

Magpie (Hawkes Bay)

Ferdinand the Bull (Taranaki)

Stu the Turbo (Manawatu)

Leo the Lion (Wellington)

Marco the Mako (Tasman)

Larry the Lamb (Canterbury)

Razor the Wild Pig (Otago)

Steve-O the Stag (Southland)

---

7 KIWI POLITICIANS WITH GOOD NAMES FOR SCRABBLE

In 2010, American analysts studied the results of the elections for Minnesota state governor for the previous 150 years. After comparing the names of the winners and losers, they discovered that, two-thirds of the time, the winner was someone whose name, when spelled out on a Scrabble board, would earn a higher score than their opponent's. An unusual name – at least, one containing less common letters of the alphabet – could earn you voter recognition. Could this theory explain our election results here?

◊ Golriz Ghahraman   34

◊ Willow-Jean Prime   32

◊ Chloe Swarbrick   30

◊ Tabuteau Fletcher   26

◊ Phil Twyford   26

- ◊ Tamati Coffey   25
- ◊ Jacinda Ardern   24

... and 3 not so good

- ◊ Paula Bennett   16
- ◊ Amy Adams   17
- ◊ Nanaia Mahuta   17

SPELLING DISASTER: 14 CURLY WINNING WORDS FROM THE NZ SPELLING BEE

Compilers of the Spelling Bee word list say they select 'useful, everyday, yet wonderful words' that the students will be able to use for the rest of their lives. Each year, hundreds of hopefuls are whittled down until one contestant remains, correctly spelling a word that could stump most of us. The champion scoops a prize of $5000 to put towards their education.

- ◊ 2005 Contiguous
- ◊ 2006 Obstreperous
- ◊ 2007 Vendetta
- ◊ 2008 Flotilla
- ◊ 2009 Iterative
- ◊ 2010 Chrysanthemum
- ◊ 2011 Conceited
- ◊ 2012 Longitudinal
- ◊ 2013 Perestroika

- ◊ 2014 Eugenics
- ◊ 2015 Meritocracy
- ◊ 2016 Ostensible
- ◊ 2017 Pusillanimous
- ◊ 2018 Frankincense

---

8 GREAT DATES FOR A NIGHT OUT DANCING

- ◊ Julz Tocker: if he recalls how it felt to be bullied about his love of dance, the *Dancing with the Stars* judge shouldn't be too savage about yours.

- ◊ Manu Vatuvei: tough but tender, if repeats his best steps from *Dancing with the Stars*, he will unbottle his emotions and let the tears flow.

- ◊ Lorde: likely to look kindly on your jerky lack of composure and coordination as exemplary interpretive dance.

- ◊ Parris Goebel: if she can choreograph for Justin Bieber and Jennifer Lopez, there's no reason not to work up a good combo for you too.

- ◊ Sir Jon Trimmer: at 80 years of age he is still dancing for the Royal NZ Ballet, though says his roles these days are 'old ladies and witches'.

- ◊ Billie Jordan of Hip-Operation Crew: well practised in accommodating the physical limitations that come with advancing years.

- ◊ Michael Parmenter: as long as he keeps his clothes on, he should be able to guide you through a sinewy, sexy tango.

- ◊ Neil Ieremia of Black Grace: so eye-catching, he'll distract anyone's attention from your lack of artistry.

… and who not to go dancing with

David Seymour: there's a disturbing possibility he might don fluorescent-coloured lycra shorts and attempt to twerk.

---

9 SONGS RENOWNED FOR BRINGING THE KIWI DAD-DANCERS OUT AT ANY DO

◊ 'Hotel California' – the Eagles

◊ 'Sweet Home Alabama' – Lynyrd Skynyrd

◊ 'Sultans of Swing' – Dire Straits

◊ 'Brown Eyed Girl' – Van Morrison

◊ 'Go Your Own Way' – Fleetwood Mac

◊ 'Sweet Child O' Mine' – Guns N' Roses

◊ 'Suspicious Minds' – Elvis Presley

◊ 'Walk of Life' – Dire Straits

◊ 'Sex on Fire' – Kings of Leon

---

9 THINGS MOTORHOMERS KNOW THAT HOME OWNERS DON'T ALWAYS APPRECIATE

◊ You can move through life very efficiently owning very little stuff.

◊ Interpersonal relationships are easier when life is less complicated.

◊ Motorhomers are not into meaningless meandering. The freedom to go wherever you please still calls for planning. (If you don't identify the right places to stay, buy groceries and dump wastewater, things can become difficult.)

◊ People who travel in motorhomes are not bludgers on society. In fact, they contribute significantly to the coffers of the communities they visit.

◊ The beds in a motorhome are perfectly comfortable. Hospitable homeowners don't need to take pity and offer their guest rooms.

◊ Most motorhomes do not travel any slower than other traffic and are no more responsible for hold-ups than other kinds of vehicles.

◊ Structure and tidiness are essential elements of happy motorhome relationships. Predictable routines for manoeuvres alleviate domestic disharmony.

◊ Motorhomers are conscious of the environment and some even initiate voluntary clean-ups.

◊ In most places where there is freedom parking, a motorhome is required to have a self-containment certificate issued by a qualified inspector. This is proof that a motorhome meets the ablutionary and sanitary needs of the occupants for a minimum of three days, without requiring external services or discharging waste.

Source: Jill Malcolm, author of *The great Kiwi Motorhome Guide*, and former editor of *Motorhomes, Caravans and Destinations magazine*.

9 WEIRD SPORTS UNLIKELY TO CATCH ON IN NEW ZEALAND

◊ Sumo from Japan

◊ Oil wrestling from Turkey

◊ Bullfighting from Spain

◊ Buzkashi from Afghanistan

◊ Camel racing from the United Arab Emirates

◊ Toe wrestling from England

◊ Elephant polo from Nepal

◊ Shin-kicking from England

◊ Wife carrying from Finland

---

7 ESSENTIAL TOOLS FOR A WEEKEND OF DIY, SELECTED BY THE RESIDENT BUILDER

◊ Hammer: Ever since our ancestors picked up a club, the humble hammer has been the cornerstone of the toolkit. A claw hammer will also help with getting those bent nails out again.

◊ Tape measure: You need to know height, width, depth, and distance, and a tape measure is the key. A folding ruler is popular with tradies, but a retractable tape measure gives more length at home.

◊ A one-metre level: Keeping on the level is impossible without this piece of toolmaking genius. A bubble floating in liquid gives you plumb and level.

◊ A set of screwdrivers: Make sure you have a selection of screwdrivers, both in size and type. Common types of screws are slotted, square drive and Pozi, and you need a screwdriver for each type.

◊ Knife: Proves its utility through its appearance in just about every tradie's toolbelt. Chippies, plumbers, electricians … everyone has one, and you should, too.

◊ Pliers: You will always need something to grab or wrench a stubborn item. A locking plier like a Visegrip gives you the bonus of extra holding power.

◊ Hand saw: Simple and effective, the traditional hand saw needs no power other than your arm and no cord to plug it in. Avoid nails, and it will stay sharp for ages.

Source: Peter Wolfkamp, Resident Builder and face of *The Block*

---

9 BEAUTIFUL BEACHES
WITH A REPUTATION FOR DANGER

Stunning, yes. But hazardous, too. People have drowned at some of the country's most picturesque beaches.

◊ Piha Beach, Auckland: On average, lifeguards rescue between 150 and 200 people a year. There are permanent rips at either end of the beach.

◊ Muriwai Beach, Auckland: Large waves attract surf lovers, but rips regularly keep lifeguards vigilant – and busy.

◊ Sunset Beach, Port Waikato: Beautiful to look at, but lifeguards were needed to rescue over 50 people in a 12-month period.

◊ Raglan, Waikato: Surfers love the world-famous long left-hand break, but between June 2016 and July 2016, lifeguards made 21 rescues and 19 'assists'.

◊ Hot Water Beach, Coromandel: It's perfectly safe to dig yourself a pool to enjoy the effects of the hot water springs. However, over the years, strong rips in the open water have claimed lives.

◊ Mt Maunganui, Bay of Plenty: When the tide is high, swimmers can be out of their depth only a few metres from shore. The potential for collision with thousands of surfboards and boogie boards is high, too.

- ◊ Whangamata, Coromandel: the area directly in front of the Surf Life Saving Club, away from the rip-plagued harbour entrance and river mouth, is the safest area for swimming.

- ◊ Marine Parade Beach, Napier: a steep seabed produces large waves that have caught swimmers unaware and led to drownings.

- ◊ St Kilda, Dunedin: classified by Surf Life Saving NZ as 'very dangerous', because of the common presence of large waves and strong rips that can defeat even strong, confident swimmers.

Source: Surf Life Saving NZ 2017 Annual Report

10 HEALTH FADS KIWIS SHOULD DROP — AND WHAT TO REPLACE THEM WITH

◊ 'No pain, no gain'	Restorative yoga
◊ Power walking	Water walking
◊ Juice cleanses	A plant-based diet
◊ WeightWatchers	Restricted hours eating
◊ Hot yoga	Yin yoga by candlelight
◊ Zumba	Adult ballet
◊ Gym mats	Shakti mats
◊ Futons	Earthing pads
◊ Boot camp	Wellness retreats
◊ Stationary bikes	E-bikes

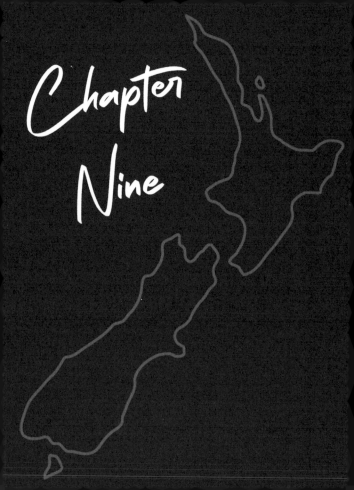

Chapter

Nine

HISTORY and HERITAGE:

Those Were the Days

DAYS THAT CHANGED NEW ZEALAND

25 April 1915: The Anzac campaign in Turkey

Australian and New Zealand troops land at Gallipoli on the coast of Turkey, ordered there by misinformed British commanders. The difficult terrain and unexpected repulsion by Turkish troops spells disaster. More than 130,000 soldiers – 2779 of them Kiwis – die during the campaign. Their courage and sacrifice under appalling conditions is recognized as the catalyst that forges a distinctly Kiwi sense of identity. From 1916 onwards, 25 April is known as Anzac Day, and every year, increasing numbers turn up at dawn ceremonies throughout New Zealand to honour the men who sacrificed their lives.

UNFORTUNATE ERROR:
8 NEW ZEALAND MYTHS THAT JUST WON'T DIE

Some things we would love to be true. It makes us feel so much better about being Kiwi. Get out the microscope, though, and some of our favourite concepts don't stand up to scrutiny.

◊ That there was human settlement in New Zealand predating the arrival of the Maori.
   A renowned expert in Pacific history from the University of Auckland, Professor Hugh Laracy, denounced such claims as 'wild speculation' that had been 'thoroughly disposed of by academic specialists'.

◊ That we should consider ourselves 'one people'.
  At Waitangi, on 6 February 1940, Sir Apirana Ngata said,
  'The message of the Maori race to you is: we want to retain
  our individuality as a race. If judged by your standards, we
  fall short. Try and look at it from the Maori standpoint … does
  it matter very much whether we square up with the Pakeha
  standards or not? Are they so very good that we should
  square up to them?'

◊ That New Zealand is 'a great place to bring up kids'.
  The Ministry of Social Development reported that, in the 12
  months ending June 2017, there were over 12,000 reported
  cases of neglect or abuse of children – either emotionally,
  physically or sexually.

◊ That we're clean and green.
  Almost half of New Zealand's lakes are classed as polluted
  by excess nutrients and many are over-run by invasive fish
  species.

◊ That there are 20 sheep per person.
  Back in 1982, we had 70 million sheep, which meant around
  22 sheep per person. In 2019, however, Statistics NZ
  reported a less embarrassing ratio of 5.6 sheep per person.

◊ That we all love rugby.
  Yes, the fans are very vocal, especially around World Cup
  time, but Sport NZ conducted a survey in 2014 and found
  that in a list of the 20 most popular sport and recreation
  activities participated in over 12 months by males, rugby
  ranked at number 16.

◊ That Chinese are buying all the property.
  Since foreign buyers have been required to have a NZ bank
  account and an IRD number, only 3 per cent of sales have
  been to buyers overseas.

◊ That Gisborne is the first place to see the sunrise each day.
  Thanks to dramatic doglegs in the International Date Line,
  that privilege goes to the island republic of Kiribati.

13 ESSENTIAL ITEMS IN ANY COLLECTION OF KIWIANA

◊ A Buzzy Bee pull-along toy

◊ A copy of the *Edmonds Cookery Book*

◊ A pair of jandals

◊ A bone pendant

◊ A pair of red socks

◊ A paua ashtray

◊ A set of rimu coasters

◊ A *Ka mate! Ka mate!* tea towel

◊ A print of Dick Frizzell's painting *Mickey to Tiki tu Meke*

◊ A Swanndri

◊ A copy of *The Little Yellow Digger* by Betty Gilderdale

◊ A plastic tiki from Air New Zealand

◊ A mini Hundertwasser flag

WE ARE THE CHAMPIONS: 11 NEW ZEALAND FIRSTS

◊ 1857: Worker unrest led by Auckland-based painter William Griffin eventuates in the adoption of the eight-hour working day on 1 September. It applies only to tradesmen and laborers, and it is not enshrined in law until later, but it is the first time the eight-hour day is adopted anywhere in the world.

◊ 1884: Referee William Harrington Atack, of Canterbury, is the first sports referee in the world to use a whistle to stop a game.

◊ 1893: New Zealand becomes the first country in the world to grant women the right to vote.

◊ 1903: On 31 March 1903, Richard Pearse flies a home-made aircraft 150 yards, making possibly the first flight in the world.

◊ 1953: Sir Edmund Hillary becomes the first person to summit Mt Everest, the world's highest mountain.

◊ 1976: Mary Ronnie is appointed New Zealand national librarian, the first female national librarian in the world.

◊ 1987: The All Blacks win the world's first Rugby World Cup.

◊ 1990: Penny Jamieson is appointed Bishop of Dunedin, becoming the first woman in the world to head an Anglican diocese.

◊ 1999: Georgina Beyer becomes the world's first openly transgender Member of Parliament.

◊ 2005: New Zealand becomes the first country in the world to have all the top jobs held by women: The Prime Minister is Helen Clark; the Governor General is Dame Silvia Cartwright, the Chief Justice is Sian Elias; the Speaker of the House is Margaret Wilson; and the Queen of New Zealand is Elizabeth II.

◊ 2012: A 4300 sq km area of sky above the Mackenzie Region in the South Island is declared an International Dark Sky Reserve, the first in the Southern Hemisphere.

---

5 Maori proverbs that pakeha philosophers probably wish they'd thought of

◊ Tama tu, tama ora; tama noho, tama mate kai.
(He who stands, lives; he who sits, perishes.)

◊ He aha te kai o te rangatira? He Korero, he korero, he korero.
(What is the food of the leader? It is knowledge. It is communication.)

◊ Kia mate ururoa, kei mate wheke.
(Fight like a shark, don't give in like an octopus.)

◊ He au kei uta e taea te karo, he au kei te moana e kore e taea.
(You may dodge smoke on land, but you cannot dodge a current at sea.)

◊ Ka pu te ruha, ka hao te rangatahi.
(The old net is cast aside, while the new net goes fishing.)

New speak: 17 concepts that spell trouble for Maori linguists

The official source of new Maori equivalents of English words in the Maori Language Commission. If you want the word for 'bitcoin', for example, or maybe 'climate change', the Commission will do an exhaustive search to check that the Maori equivalent doesn't already exist. If it doesn't, a new word will be coined and then undergo a lengthy peer review before it is entered into an electronic database of neologisms. A lot of modern concepts could tax the skills of even the cleverest linguist. Don't expect a decision soon on any of the following:

◊ Bromance

◊ Crowdsourcing

◊ F-bomb

◊ To friend-zone someone

◊ Helicopter parent

◊ Nanny state

- ◊ Lifestyle blogging
- ◊ Man cave
- ◊ Manspreading
- ◊ Muffin top
- ◊ Peak cow
- ◊ Reality TV
- ◊ Side boob
- ◊ Twerking
- ◊ Virtue signalling
- ◊ Vocal fry
- ◊ X-factor

...and 10 words that have been recently introduced

- ◊ Haukori angi (cardio funk)
- ◊ Miraka pini (soy milk)
- ◊ Mowai (flat white)
- ◊ Waea pukoro (mobile phone)
- ◊ Haumanu a-kakara (aromatherapy)
- ◊ Patuhi (to text)
- ◊ Mauiui whaiaro rua (bipolar disorder)
- ◊ Tunga waka whaikaha (disability parking)
- ◊ Punaha kimi ahunga (global positioning system)
- ◊ Ahokore (wi-fi)

14 HERITAGE MOMENTS

Some moments mark a watershed, introducing a new practice or attitude that will change 'the Kiwi way' forever.

◊ 15 June 1959: Cold War era prejudice means the North American market is failing to see the appeal of 'Chinese gooseberries'. At a management meeting of Turners and Growers, Jack Turner proposes that 'kiwifruit' might be a more politically digestible name. The industry adopts the new name nationwide, and the 'hairy berry' soon becomes a nice little export earner.

◊ 6 March 1966: The first episode of *Country Calendar* screens. It includes a less-than-riveting report on market prices and an interview with the chairman of the Meat Board, shot in the studio, with the presenter and interviewee wearing un-rural suits and ties. However, the programme endures, and it now comes second only to *Coronation Street* as the world's longest-running TV programme.

◊ 30 June 1975: TV2 begins broadcasting, and, during its first year, introduces the Goodnight Kiwi for its closedown. Each night, the appealing little Kiwi turns out the studio lights, places the empty milk bottle by the door, and catches a lift up to the satellite dish where his bed is. Nobody minds that he sleeps with The Cat.

◊ 18 March 1984: 'Poi E', sung by the Patea Maori Club, hits number one on the pop charts and stays there for four consecutive weeks. By the end of 1984, it has become the year's biggest selling single, outselling all international recording artists. It enjoys a resurgence after Taiki Waititi's film *Boy* is released.

◊ 10 September 1984: A dawn ceremony is held in front of the Metropolitan Museum of Art for the opening of *Te Maori*. The exhibition is the first occasion on which Maori objects and artefacts are shown internationally as art, and the event is reported on the front page of the *New York Times*. Never again will there be any excuse for cultural cringe.

◊ 4 February 1985: David Lange tells the Americans that USS *Buchanan* – a US ship with potential nuclear capability – is not welcome in our harbours. It is the day that New Zealand effectively becomes nuclear free. The Nuclear Free Zone legislation is brought into being within two years.

◊ 26 October 1985: Before the All Blacks test against Argentina, Buck Shelford leads a revitalized haka that, under his tuition, has become a powerful psychological weapon. Previous performances have been woefully inadequate – inaccurate, embarrassing and lacklustre. From this moment, the power and significance of the haka will be respected worldwide.

◊ 14 December 1991: Mt Cook/Aoraki loses its top. Ice and rocks tumble down its slopes, creating vibrations that are felt as far away as Wellington. Kiwis awake to the news that the summit of their highest mountain has dropped by 10 metres.

◊ 6 November 1993: In a referendum on the country's electoral system, 54 per cent of voters opt for Mixed-Member Proportional Representation (MMP) to replace First Past the Post (FPP). The new system will lead to the emergence of Winston Peters, leader of New Zealand First, as the quirky, even improbable, 'kingmaker'.

◊ 9 October 1999: Hinewehi Mohi is in London to promote her Oceania album when she is asked to sing the national anthem at Twickenham before the New Zealand-England World Cup game. She does so – in Maori. Since then, we have always sung the first verse in te reo.

◊ 27 August 2002: John Clarke gifts Fred Dagg's mismatched Skellerup gumboots and his black shearer's singlet to Te Papa Museum. Fred Dagg had been beloved by the nation since 1973, when he was introduced to viewers of the TV current affairs show *Gallery* and on a spoof episode of *Country Calendar*.

◇ 1 July 2007: KiwiSaver is introduced as a voluntary work-based savings scheme designed to help people save for retirement. By October 2017, 2.8 million individuals have enrolled in KiwiSaver.

◇ 1 December 2010: The *Oxford English Dictionary* launches a new online edition and unequivocally declares that the pavlova, a culinary icon, was invented in New Zealand. The recipe, the *OED* points out, was introduced to the world in a book published in 1927 by a Kiwi company, Davis Gelatine. This should have put an end to a long-standing trans-Tasman rivalry, but sometimes Aussies get confused about what's theirs and what's ours.

◇ 15 March 2019: Following terrorist attacks on two Christchurch mosques in which 50 people are slain, Jacinda Ardern creates a shift in the way we view our Muslim community. We all call New Zealand home, she reminds us, and 'They Are Us' temporarily becomes a grieving nation's mantra.

20 CLASSIC KIWI RIVALRIES

◇ Waitangi Day v Anzac Day

◇ Sauvignon blanc v Chardonnay

◇ Air New Zealand v Jetstar

◇ Mono hull v Multi hull

◇ Red peak v Southern cross

◇ Smacking v Time out

◇ Spark v Vodafone

◊ Christmas turkey v Beach barbecue

◊ Sky TV v Netflix

◊ Labour v National

◊ Fracking v Greenpeace

◊ Cycle lanes v Car lanes

◊ Auction v Asking price

◊ Whittaker's v Cadbury's

◊ Uber v Traditional taxis

◊ Fluoridated v Non-fluoridated

◊ Decriminalisation v Legalisation

◊ *Seven Sharp* v *The Project*

◊ Leighton Smith v manmade global warming

◊ New Zealand v Australia

ART APPRECIATION: 10 ITEMS TO SAVE IF TE PAPA WERE ON FIRE

Nobody who works at the Museum of New Zealand Te Papa Tongarewa could possibly select just 10 treasures to save from among the 2.5 million items in Te Papa's collections. But to an independent observer, certain things would stand out for immediate rescue:

◊ Michael Parekowhai's carved red Steinway concert grand piano, called *He Korero Purakau mo te Awanui o Te Motu: Story of a New Zealand River*. It took more than 10 years to create, using ivory, brass, lacquer, steel, ebony, paua shell, resin, and mother of pearl, and cost Te Papa around $1.5 million.

◊ Colin McCahon's 1947 painting *Angel of the Annunciation*, which shows Mary receiving the news of her miraculous pregnancy from the Angel Gabriel against a recognisable depiction of the Nelson Hills and the Tahunanui golf clubhouse.

◊ The Olympic gold medal that Peter Snell won in the 800 m race at the Rome Olympics in 1960. He was only 21 years of age at the time and became an instant national celebrity. So many fans touched the medal that some of the medal's gilt has worn off.

◊ The hei tiki that belonged to Te Paea Hinerangi, known as Guide Sophia, who lived in the Rotorua area from the 1870s to the early 1900s. For 16 years, Guide Sophia took tourists to see the Pink and White Terraces at the foot of Mt Tarawera. In May 1886, she saw the water level in the lake suddenly fall and then rise again, before a canoe appeared in the distance. When the canoe came closer, she saw 13 people in it, all with dogs' heads. A few days later, on 10 June 1886, Mount Tarawera erupted and the famous terraces were destroyed.

◊ The diary of Captain EP Cox, Wellington Infantry Battalion, written while on service in Gallipoli, 1915. The entries are made in pencil on each of the 204 loose pages. On Sunday, 15 April 1915, Cox wrote: 'It is a most glorious morning and perfectly calm at sea. Everyone on board is in high spirits and eagerly awaits coming events'.

◊ The record-breaking Britten V-1000 motorbike, a stunning example of Kiwi ingenuity. Its innovative styling – including the use of carbon fibre in its structure – was the inspiration of John Britten, a mechanical engineer from Christchurch, whose intention was to make the fastest four-stroke bike in the world. It is the second of only 10 bikes ever made and holds four official world speed records, all gained in 1993.

◊ The skeleton of Phar Lap, champion thoroughbred racehorse who won the Melbourne Cup on 4 November 1930. Australian attempts to appropriate him notwithstanding – his skin is exhibited at Melbourne's Museum Victoria, and his large heart at the National Museum of Australia in Canberra – Phar Lap was Kiwi-bred, foaled near Timaru in 1926.

◊ The colossal squid, the largest intact example ever found and the only one of its kind on display in the world. The female squid, which is 5.4 m long, was collected by commercial fishers in the Ross Sea, Antarctica, in 2003. Her eyes are as big as basketballs.

◊ The greenstone mere (weapon) Tuhiwai, which was given to Te Rauparaha in exchange for a war canoe. The mere was used by Te Rangihaeata to execute European prisoners as utu for the death of his wife during the conflict at Wairau in 1843.

◊ The ball from the rugby game played between New Zealand and South Africa at Eden Park, Auckland, on 1 September 1956. A win meant the All Blacks could claim an at-home test series victory against the Springboks for the first time. Peter Jones scored the winning try and fullback Don 'The Boot' Clarke converted it.
After the match, Jones's memorable reaction was broadcast live on national radio: 'I hope I never have to play in a tougher game than what I did today', he said. 'I'm absolutely buggered.'

What New Zealand politicians said when 6 prominent foreigners died

◊ Jim Bolger on Diana, Princess of Wales (d. 31 August 1997): 'All over the world people felt they had a share in her life, and that was perhaps the explanation both of her charm and, ultimately, her tragedy.'

◊ Jim Bolger on Mother Teresa (d. 5 September 1997): 'Mother Teresa was truly an Angel of Mercy, working tirelessly for nearly 50 years to restore dignity and hope to the poor, destitute and dying. She believed there was no worse disease than that of feeling unwanted. She was truly Christian love in action. Her goodness and compassion will forever be a guiding light to us all.'

◊ Helen Clark on Ronald Reagan (d. 5 June 2004): 'His greatest gift was his ability to communicate, and he always conveyed a sense of optimism about his country and its people.'

◊ Winston Peters on Pope John Paul II (d. 2 April 2005): 'During a period when hedonism and materialism held sway, he was guided by ethical and moral principles alone. Whilst we may not all have agreed with all his beliefs, no one could doubt the steeliness and fortitude with which he held his beliefs and the profound effect he had upon the century in which he lived.'

◊ Bill English on Nelson Mandela (d. 5 December 2013): 'Nelson Mandela's passing will cast a long shadow. His place in history is unassailable. We can honour his legacy by supporting South Africa to stay on Mr Mandela's path of forgiveness, freedom and prosperity.'

◊ Annette King on Gough Whitlam (d. 21 October 2014): 'He was 1.94 metres tall, he had a flowing mop of silver hair and a big booming voice, and his oratory was spellbinding.

When he was asked what his plans were for the next stage, his afterlife, he replied, of a possible meeting with his maker: "You can be sure of one thing – I shall treat Him as an equal".'

Why, thank you? 11 quirky gifts
Kiwis gave the Royals

◊ 1953: The Queen (for Princess Anne) – a plastic model of a Maori woman and child.

◊ 1981: Prince Charles and Diana – a quantity of all-wool broadloom carpet ('textured but not patterned'), eventually laid at the couple's country home in Gloucestershire.

◊ 2002: The Queen – five volumes of the *Dictionary of New Zealand Biography,* the five volumes of *Nga tangata taumata rau,* a CD marking the online publication of the dictionary's website, and the *New Zealand Historical Atlas,* all in a New Zealand timber case.

◊ 2005: Prince Charles – a blown albatross egg from the Albatross Centre in Dunedin.

◊ 2005: Prince William of Wales – 48 letters from children, given by Arrowtown Primary School.

◊ 2011: William and Kate, Duke and Duchess of Cambridge, for their wedding – a donation to the Christchurch Earthquake Appeal.

◊ 2013: Prince George – a 'Filmy Fern' lace shawl designed by Margaret Stove and handknitted by Cynthia Read.

◊ 2014: Kate – a single stem red rose from Helen Tuck of Tauranga.

◊ 2015: Princes Charles – a packet of fairy dust.

◊ 2015: Camilla, Duchess of Cambridge – a quilt decorated with Kiwiana icons, made by inmates of Arohata Prison.

◊ 2018: Prince Harry and Meghan Markle – an All Blacks onesie for their first baby, presented by a fan during the royal walkabout at Auckland's Viaduct Harbour.

---

9 THINGS YOU PROBABLY DIDN'T KNOW ABOUT THE BEEHIVE

◊ The architect, Sir Basil Spence, apparently used a pencil to sketch what would become known as the Beehive on the back of a napkin during a dinner with Prime Minister Keith Holyoake in 1964.

◊ There are 1513 windows in the Beehive.

◊ There is a gym and swimming pool in the Beehive.

◊ The distance from the podium on which the Beehive stands to the top of its flagpole is 72 metres.

◊ The Beehive has, since 1992, featured as part of the design of the New Zealand $20 note.

◊ In 2015, Heritage New Zealand assigned the Beehive the highest rating for a historic place: Category 1.

◊ The site the Beehive occupies was initially the site of the house of Colonel William Wakefield, one of the earliest European settlers at Port Nicholson (Wellington) and Principal Agent for the New Zealand Company in New Zealand.

◊ Cabinet usually meets on Mondays in the Cabinet room on the tenth floor of the Beehive.

◊ The National Crisis Management Centre is located in the Beehive basement and is designed for maximum self-sustainability in the event of a major Wellington earthquake.

KIWISPEAK: 15 BITS OF LOCAL LINGO
THAT HAVE BAFFLED A FEW FOREIGN TOURISTS

◊ Across the Ditch: over the Tasman Sea (to Australia)

◊ Booze bus: the roadside checkpoint where police stop drivers to see if they blow over the limit for alcohol

◊ Chateau cardboard: wine sold in a cardboard box; regarded as a last resort for thirsty picnickers

◊ Couch kumara: a person who sits on the couch watching TV for hour after hour

◊ Extra curly: a suitable response from somebody who's asked how they're going and who feels particularly well

◊ Fart tax: a tax proposed by politicians and rejected by farmers

◊ To go hard out: to put the utmost effort into anything

◊ Maussie: a Maori who lives in Australia

◊ Kwaussie: an Australian-based Kiwi, like Barnaby Joyce – who, incidentally, had to resign his deputy prime ministership because of it

◊ Munted: broken or ruined

◊ She'll be right: everything will be okay

◊ To take an early shower: to be sent off the field for unsporting behaviour, indicated by the ref holding up a red card

◊ To pack a sad: to wallow in unhappiness, to be upset

◊ To handle the jandal: to deal with a situation

◊ A tiki tour: an unnecessarily long way from Point A to Point B

Hellfire and damnation:
7 inflammatory stances of the Destiny Church

◊ The church's 'prosperity theology', whereby members are encouraged to donate 10 per cent of every dollar they earn to the church. Many are offended by the Tamakis' opulent lifestyle, which includes Mercedes-Benz cars, a Harley Davidson motorbike, a boat, first-class overseas travel, and a home with spa and heated pool purchased for $1.58 million. Tamaki has said 'You've really got nothing until people get jealous around you.'

◊ Despite preaching sexual abstinence for young people in a bid to curb abortion, teenage pregnancy and the spread of STDs, the church launches a 2018 recruitment drive based on its pastor's 'hotness'. In a Facebook listing for Bishop Brian Tamaki Ministries, Tamaki's beaming face looms large adjacent to the caption 'Super-size your faith in a hot church with a hot preacher!'

◊ During a sermon on 16 November 2016, Brian Tamaki blames homosexuals and murderers for the 2010 and 2011 Christchurch earthquakes. 'The earth can speak. Leviticus says that the earth convulses under the weight of certain human sin,' he declares.

◊ On 24 October 2009, 700 male members of the church are handpicked to be Brian Tamaki's 'spiritual sons'. A special ceremony is held, during which these newly proclaimed 'sons' swear loyalty and obedience – 'an irrevocable, undissolvable oath of commitment' – to the preacher. Each 'son' is given a 'covenant ring' in return for promising to quote Tamaki in favourable terms as often as possible and to bestow gifts upon him on special occasions.

◊ In August 2004, Destiny members march on Parliament to protest civil unions legislation. Their slogan is 'Enough is Enough' and Tamaki decries what he sees as the government's 'radical homosexual agenda'. Media respond to the black T-shirts and trackpants worn by many of the marchers by comparing the protesters with Nazi stormtroopers.

◊ At a 2003 Destiny Church conference, Tamaki prophesies that, 'by the time we hit our tenth anniversary [in 2008] … we will be ruling the nation … this will be the first nation historically in the world to be under the governance of God'. By 2018, such talk has been replaced by invitations to purchase tickets for $150 per person to a ball to celebrate Tamaki's sixtieth birthday.

◊ On 21 March 2019, Tamaki tweets his anger that the Islamic call to prayer will be broadcast during a ceremony to remember the victims of the Christchurch mosque attacks. 'PM Jacinda Ardern has abused her Prime Ministerial decree in allowing "Allah as the only true God" to be sounded in Muslim prayer across the air waves in our nation tomorrow,' he says. 'This is offensive to all true Christians in Aotearoa. Our national identity is at stake.'

Yeah, nah.

KIWI KA PAI: 15 REASONS WE'RE HAPPY
IN OUR OWN SKIN

In July 2017, Statistics NZ reported that Kiwis, generally, were satisfied with life. Around 83 per cent of us rated our overall satisfaction as 7 or above on the 0–10 scale, and we reported a strong sense of belonging to New Zealand. It's not hard to see why.

◊ The NZ passport opens the door to 168 countries without the need for a visa, and the rest of the world seems happy to see us. Nobody puts us on a boat and sends us back before we've even landed.

◊ The neighbours, bless 'em, are reasonably friendly. Well, we haven't actually declared outright war against each other and as long as we continue to keep our grasp on the Bledisloe Cup, things should remain calm.

◊ We can stretch out. We're bigger than the UK, with only 7 per cent of their population.

◊ In terms of plain old decency, we are on top of our game, ranking with the best in the world in the 2018 Corruption Perceptions Index published by Transparency International. Denmark has snatched the lead, but we come in a very respectable second.

◊ There are plenty of Pacific island holiday spots within coo-ee. You can barely get through your meal and a glass of sauvignon blanc before landing.

◊ A 'fair go' is the nationwide mantra. Road rages and consumer rip-offs do happen, but they're fairly promptly and unceremoniously sorted.

◊ You might bump into a weta in your outdoor shed, but you won't stand on any snakes.

◊ We've got a very smart national airline to take us on our overseas outings.

◊ We've got at least one national sports team to be proud of. Maybe more.

◊ There is no compulsory military service.

◊ The beach is never far away. The farthest you can get from the coastline is 120 km. In some parts of the US, you'd have to travel 20 times that distance before dipping your toe in the ocean.

◊ Health care and education are available for next to nothing.

◊ We might get four seasons in one day, but we don't have to add or remove endless layers of clothing to deal with it. The difference between the average daily high and the average daily low in most locations is less than 10° Celsius.

◊ The food and wine are good. So is the coffee.

◊ We've got everything we need right here, thank you.

Kia ora!